EMBRA

SUPER HUMAN

**A Guide To Unlocking Your Higher Self Through
Meditation & Science**

ARF

Contents

Chapter – 1 1

The birth of a new being 1

Forgiveness is a Super Power 28

Dark Night of Your Soul...................................37

What Qualifies as a Superhuman?....................44

Chapter - 2 52

Conscious Mind and The Subconscious Mind 52

Brain and The Heart Connection 63

The power of thought on our brain and body 72

The Science of Cymatics and Water.................78

Chapter - 3 80

What Is Quantum Science, And How Does It Work? 80

Brain Waves and Their Key to Embracing The
Superhuman 91

The Power of Emotion and Belief....................94

Law of Cause and Effect in Regards to Pain &
Healing..113

Chapter - 4 117

Neurolinguistic Programming (Nlp)............117

Epigenetics 127

Gratitude, and The Elevated Emotions Experiment 137

Superhuman and The Science of The Placebo Effect ..144

Chapter - 5 .... **151**

What Is Meditation 151

What is Personalized Meditation? 171

René Peoch's 'The Great Experiment' 176

Designing Your Personalised Meditation 180

Epilogue **190**

Chapter – 1

The birth of a new being

"Everything in this universe is interconnected with synchrony, hence giving divine power to the expression of the omnipresent source, giving the sense to comprehend divine wisdom and knowledge. Memory starts to fade away, and knowing begins the play."

~ Arf.

It was late evening during the peak of summer; I was seated in my room in despair, looking at every corner of the green and white walls and wondering what happened to my life. The beautiful room that once felt so pleasant seemed to be breaking on my head, and the pain of every loss I had faced was drooling down my throat, and there seemed absolutely no way out. It was already three weeks of being locked up in one room that only bread misery, pain and cries, which plunged my lungs upside down, thinking and feeling desperate, angry, scared, traumatized and severely depressed. It had been long since my mind started convincing me to leave this body, to end all miseries once and for all, and the day was today, to finally leave; my mind convinced me about the loss my family would face after I left and that my parents would be well taken care of by my sisters and it will be long before any of my family would reach back to my home town from another country to find no trace of me. Soon I would become a nobody in this world. The suicidal thought was very dominant and convincing that I decided to leave without a note and use the easiest mode of leaving this body by hanging it. As I gathered the needed material to support my weight, something deep down told me with a soothing voice, before you leave, why don't you cherish all the beautiful memories you have had with people you loved and then while holding all the beautiful memories in your heart, leave. As soothing as the voice was, it held a certain type of command. As I sat down on my bed with my feet hanging down to the ground, I lay my head on my knees and thought to myself, the loss of losing a loved one to a severe psychological illness, to the loss of losing the right over my child to the loss of drowning every saved penny of my hard-earned money into a start-up, growled at me and the possibility of thinking some beautiful memory seemed no option. As I lay my head on my knees, I began to cry intensely and felt the entire pain all over again, the flashback of the entire misery wrapped all around me, and I cried almost till I fell unconscious. Then a voice gently asked me to get up and look at myself in the mirror in my wardrobe. I got up from my bed and walked to my wardrobe and saw my face all swelled up with veins bulging out on my forehead and with eyes that turned blood red; it seemed like I saw the most shattered version of myself in the mirror. I looked at myself for a few minutes till I couldn't look anymore and turned around and witnessed another me sleeping on the bed, or perhaps dead on the bed. I still don't know who was the real me that night. Was it me looking at myself in the mirror or the one on the bed, or was that a dream? That remains a mystery.

The next day I woke up on my bed and looked around the room; the bright sunlight hitting my face on a summer morning seemed like the best experience of my life. I sat there on my bed with my eyes closed, absorbing the sunlight, and that is when an intuitive message downloaded into my mind saying my healing has begun and all of that misery is history, and the voice said: "Someone will come and simply take you away from this mess."

Keeping my eyes closed for the first time in my life felt like eternal bliss, and I kept my eyes closed, further dissolving into the experience. To my surprise, in a few minutes, someone knocked on my door. I got up and opened the door to see my cousin looking at me with a stressed-out face and just expressed five words, "Let's get out of here!"

He started packing my bags and locked up my apartment, and took me to his beautiful place for a change. In the evening, as I relaxed on his couch, I scrolled through my Facebook, and I kept on seeing random photos and videos of the Himalayas, the snow-capped mountain peaks (three to be precise), the trees, the rivers, coffee in a white cup and felt a cold and comfortable breeze brush my face [could have been the AC though, but the feeling was real]. Looking at this amount of nature simply on my phone never made me have a heartthrob before. However, the evening passed, and I went to a gas station with my cousin in his car for a refuel. I had a picture flash on my mind screen of an unknown hand getting stuck in a trunk hatch, and just before we left the gas station, I saw someone getting their fingers stuck in their trunk hatch while closing it carelessly, and I smiled thinking how coincidental.

When you finally find your way home, the definition of home changes

~ Arf

Every time I scrolled through my phone, I saw more and more nature, and it gave me a different sense of peace. I eventually started watching videos of mountains, rivers and trees on a loop for days on my cousin's lavish TV screen. One day my father called me up from abroad and asked me about my well-being and offered me a lifetime deal of sponsoring a vacation anywhere, I wanted to go, and without doubt, I chose the Himalayas!

As I reached a remote tourist town in the Himalayan region, I found a beautiful wooden cottage that was up on a mountaintop at an unbelievably low price, and the owner of the cottage invited me down to his place to wind up the rental documentation part and the payment. As I reached his house, he asked me to have a seat on his balcony, and as I sat on a beautiful old wooden chair, I got mesmerized looking at the view from there; it captured 'three' snow-capped mountain tops with clouds crashing into them, rivers crisscrossing each other with such grace and a cold, gentle breeze brushing my face, and I turned around to the voice of my cottage owner, to see him offering me a cup of coffee, precisely in a white colour cup!

Many such experiences started to happen at a faster pace, and I started to literally notice them and found myself incapable of putting them into the loose box of coincidences, and I couldn't stop and think, why do I know things beforehand? Why am I getting connected to nature so deeply? Why am I enjoying the silence within? [like this had never happened before] A thousand whys dug me into a well of curiosity. A thirst to know what happened? What changed within me?

As the pleasure of keeping these eyes closed reached its heights, I surrendered myself to the forests in the Himalayan mountains, almost forgetting who I once was and dissolving myself into the wilderness of nature and sat down with my eyes closed for hours on end every day for months, then, my mind started talking to me, the internet in my brain got a 5g upgrade. Still, this time it was not the same voice I had in my mind as earlier; this voice appeared more confident, more powerful, a voice that seemed like a higher self or the divine self. The structure of my face and body began to look healthier and more rejuvenated, and I lost all the unhealthy weight I had on me for years without even realizing it (I lost 14kgs in two months); the quality of my sleep increased immensely and this amount of energy I haven't felt in my body probably since childhood.

The moment of meditativeness is the biggest present one can receive; perhaps that's why the capability of being in the present moment is a present or a gift by itself

~Arf.

One beautiful morning as I opened my eyes, hearing the beautiful sounds of birds chirping, the river flowing in my backyard and seeing the beautiful sunlight pierce through the wooden walls of my room and yet feeling the cosy chill on my feet, I got down the bed feeling blissed and blessed as all these mornings in the Himalayan mountains were, I walked towards my big balcony that opened into the first floor of my cottage overlooking the backyard, I saw these three mountain peaks snow-capped. The clouds crashing into them at my eye level and feeling the cold breeze that carried the smell of the apple farms all around, blending with warm sun rays on my skin, made me sit with my eyes closed on a comfortable cane sofa and take a deep dive into my inner world of meditativeness. As I spent some time keeping my eyes closed and taking some deep, powerful breaths, a vision popped up on my mind screen of a white woman roughly in her 40s talking to me, and expressing the power of my inner being, in a slight European accent and with a warm smile, she said, "you have the power to control all the elements of nature in you, as it came to you as a "present" and in the present lies a potential with which you can change the entire course of this world to peace and harmony. It's the light you emit while harnessing the present, which is enough to heal every living and non-living being around you". As I sat still and disconnected from the mesmerizing view of the three snow-capped mountains that I witnessed just before closing my eyes, I remained confused as my rational mind sneaked in, as judgment took over, left me analysing the message that was so deep and thinking it probably was a movie clip perhaps stored in my subconscious mind that just randomly popped up while diving deep. I said to myself let's call this meditation off and abruptly opened my eyes. To my surprise and a sweet shock, once I opened my eyes, I saw four dogs just sitting and relaxing, three monkeys, two parrots (on a tree right next to me) and a cow right down in my backyard simply sitting and relaxing and at peace with each other's company, it rather felt as if they were absorbing something pleasant. This had never actually happened before, especially in my backyard vicinity right under my big balcony. I felt and thought how beautiful can this be, of witnessing all this, but I rarely thought it could be a message and got up to get ready for my morning walk into the forest. I slipped into my favourite haram pants, got my leather jacket and boots, grabbed my sunglasses and walked into the wilderness bliss of the forest.

As I walked for half an hour, dosing myself in the lush green energy of the forest, I saw a mother and a toddler (roughly a two year one) walking on the same pathway as mine but coming from the opposite side. From my dark sunglasses, my eyes got mesmerized looking into the blue eyes of the toddler from a distance; the intensity of divinity my heart was feeling in the moment looking into the eyes of that toddler while he looked right back into my dark sunglasses as if he could see my eyes is still inexpressible. It felt like we both knew we were destined to cross this path today and exchange a subtle message from the divine. While this moment felt everlasting, the mother, the toddler and I reached a closer point of crossing each other and heading in the opposite direction of the wild forest. The toddler, who was still in eye contact with me, very softly hit his tiny foot on a small round rock and fell right on his face into the muddy ground. I stopped and immediately sat on my knee with some guilt, mystically knowing the mother knew her baby and I were entangled in eye contact before he toppled. I picked up the baby toddler from the ground and made him stand while cleaning the mud on his clothes and a little bit on his nose (his cute little face, blushing white skin, and pure and divine blue eyes can never be forgotten), I noticed the mother looking at me with a smile. I with that guilt immediately told her sorry for what just happened, and she continued to smile at me and said, "No, it was not your fault, it's the light you have around you that captured my baby's attention, and it is a blessing," saying this with a beautiful smile she walked away with her adorable little baby.

I slowly walked my path in the forest with a feeling of curiosity and a feeling of something that I had ignored today morning. I took an abrupt stop and turned around to see if I could still see the mother and the toddler, and I realized they had walked far away by then and turned back around and stood right at that spot, realizing the toddler's mother I had just crossed path with looked like a white woman, approximately forty years in age, spoke exactly in the same European English accent as the vision I had received in the morning meditation. I smiled at myself and thought as I continued to walk in the beautiful forest, I truly have the power to harness the five elements of life (water, air, earth, fire and ether), but I wondered how this would ever be of any relevance to me, but at the moment, I felt extremely strong and empowered, felt like at this moment if I wish to conquer this world, I could!

After returning to my hometown almost after a year of being in the mountains, I could barely stay outdoors in the urban city and society I belonged to. It felt as if I was an alien in this world; no one out there felt real; it became evident to see people just playing roles in life, they were all masking themselves to some eternal truths in ignorance, and all were living in their self-made misery, and the worst part was that none of the close ones I witnessed was even ready to heal, as they got so much engraved in their miseries, it felt like misery became a part of their life and identity. Everyone had a mask to wear, one for work, one for parties and social gatherings, one for family, one for the poor, one for the rich and so on, and have forgotten their true selves. My heart ached to heal everyone, with the present or the gift I found within me, but then one day realized the higher truth about healing others; I understood healing is a gift, a gift a healer gives to the healed, and this transaction of healing will only happen when the other wants it from you or in rare cases you are destined to heal the other. It reminded me of my puppy love story when my teenage girlfriend wanted to give me a gift, and I did not accept it, so she threw it away. What I mean by this is it's a gift; it can be given only if the other is ready to accept or receive it.

After a few days of staying amid the urban toxicity, I decided to move to a friend's farmhouse that was in the suburbs, a big and lavish luxury in the middle of a big farm. I felt the amount of nature, and the greenery around that place was what had called me there. As I was chilling, relaxing and exploring the inner me in that lush nature one evening, my friend came down to see me; he came down in a taxi as he had crashed his new Suzuki car into the divider by accident that afternoon, but gracefully escaped scratch less and not harming anyone around. He was an intelligent and humorous young man who sat silently that day on the other side of the space we used to chill at. As I sat and looked at him with compassion and empathy, I had a voice in me revealing.

"Bad things happen to good people for great reasons"

~ *Arf*

However, he happened to become more successful in what he was doing after this accident and happened to buy a Jaguar and an Audi, both together, well that is still not my point, but it is important to understand that if you are someone who is good at heart, who desires the best for everyone around you, who never cheats or betrays any one, be rest assured, everything that happens in your life is in your favour and that is the law of nature, may be an accident like this, you have saved someone losing their life on the next junction if you would have probably crashed there, or your family member might have taken your car out for a drive and have a fatal accident(if the car was not in the garage getting fixed) and there can be a million different reasons that may be out of our sense of perception and awareness, but the ultimate truth is this if you are a good person by heart, the universe or god conspires in your favour to protect you and to bless you even more.

As I sat one evening around 10:00 p.m. on a beautiful wing chair in the farmhouse all alone, I tumbled over the vision that I had in the Himalayas about the forty-year-old European woman who said that I possessed the power to harness the five elements of life and still wondered what relevance it could hold in my life. I sat down in a semi drowsy state, talking to my intuitive mind and asking myself to reveal deeper what it meant about the message I had visioned months back, and relaxed my body and dosed off to sleep on that wing chair. I happened to wake up at 3:30 a.m. almost unintentionally; I got up and walked towards the sit-out area outdoors next to the pool where I normally sat to meditate. I sat there feeling as if I had a deep and sound sleep, and now I am fresh to start the day. I sat there looking at the glittering stars, hearing the wind dance with the beautiful trees hidden in the dark; I felt peace wrap all around me and felt as if something had been answered.

The voice in me that always inspired me to sit with my eyes closed today asked me to browse YouTube on my laptop. As I saw my laptop right across, I opened it and connected the charger and began to browse at four in the morning. Which felt a little uneasy and unusual, but I continued to browse as if someone else had taken the wheel. I stopped over automatically at a video seminar of four hours hosted by America's leading scientist and author, Gregg Braden. It felt like the universe, or God introduced me to this great man's work and research. By eight in the morning, I was sitting with a sweet shock, thinking about the European lady in my dream who expressed my inner power, and now I began contemplating all this science behind it. The realization that came to me that morning was the most powerful lesson of my life; the great scientist could explain and prove his work in just four words by the end.

"Feeling is the prayer."

~ *Gregg Braden*

The massive amount of energy our heart produces when we are in deep states of empathy, joy and compassion or the energy we harness being meditative is the key to harnessing the five elements and creating anything in life; this energy that the heart creates referred to as a feeling is enough to get all the elements of this physical life in your conscious control. By physical life, I mean you have the capability to manifest anything you desire in life, be it financial abundance or healing a deadly disease in your body, or it is about praying rain when there is a need. None are beyond the capabilities of a human mind that learned to harness the power of the present moment.

Sir Gregg Braden expressed the story of meeting his Native American neighbour from where he lived in the high deserts of New Mexico back in the early 1990s. The story goes like this, Sir Gregg was invited by his neighbour David for an ancient ritual practised by the Native American tribes to manifest rain and asked him if he would like to come with him to pray for rain as New Mexico was hitting drought for that summer. He followed his neighbour to a place with stones kept in a circle and was told by his neighbour that this circle was a sacred space for the tribal people to pray. Gregg was not ready for what he saw; he says, I was thinking there were going to be some Native Americans with feathers around their heads, dancing, chanting, singing and stuff, and that's not what happened at all. The neighbour removed his shoes from the circle and, with his naked feet, stepped into the circle and honoured his past and honoured his ancestors and held his hands with both palms touching each other just for twenty seconds and opened his eyes.

As Gregg looked at him, he smiled and said I am hungry; let's go get some food. Gregg got surprised and asked him; I thought we were going to pray for rain. He smiled and said, "If we prayed for rain, rain would never happen. The moment you ask for something, you acknowledge it is not here now. If you are praying that God please give us rain, or please give me healing or please find me my soulmate, you are acknowledging you don't have it right now. Then Gregg asked his friend David, if you did not pray for rain with both your palms joined in that sacred circle of stones, what did you do? He said; when I closed my eyes, I felt as if the rain had already happened. He said, I felt my naked feet in the mud with rain water, and I smelled the fragrance of rain, he said I felt the feeling of how it feels when running across a corn field in the village when it is raining heavily, and then I gave gratitude and thanks for the rain as if it has already happened. That evening, as the sun was setting, Gregg saw clouds, clouds coming from every direction and becoming darker, and it started to rain, rain so hard that it continued through to the next day and the next day, and I thought to myself, "well that is a prayer well answered by God."

The key to effective prayer is simple; as I learnt and experienced, it is just feeling and believing as if it has already happened, not from a place of lack or victimization but from gratitude, contentment and satisfaction.

After spending a few months in the beautiful big farmhouse, my heart craved more nature; this time, it craved the beaches, and I knew exactly what had to be done. I started watching more videos of nature involving beaches and sea shores, as I wanted to experience some clean beaches, unlike a lot of public beaches here in India; I watched videos of beautiful clean beaches from across the globe and got the hang of those videos in my head and sat down with my eyes closed. I visualized staying at the beach, sleeping every night hearing the waves crash, waking up every morning hearing the waves crash, feeling the sensation of humidity and cold air brushing my face and feeling how it would be like to feel the cold waters crashing into my feet at 2:00 a.m. on a wintery night on a full moon and felt grateful as if I am already staying at the beach. I did this so religiously for a few nights before I slept, and after a week or ten days, my friend came over to see me. He asked me about my well-being and if I needed anything at the farmhouse and then slipped into a conversation expressing, how he was done with the city life and wanted to take a break from his work and asked me where do you think we should go for such a break? Without a doubt, I told him, let's go to Goa (a famous beach tourism destination in India).

We decided to see what we had in our pockets and left for the place that called us. We reached a beach in the south of Goa called Agonda. After reaching Agonda, we realized it was the sixth most clean beach in all of Asia. I said to myself, what a blessing. After staying at the beach for a few days, we decided to work while we vacationed, as this is the best combination anybody would ever want to experience, and we rented out a restaurant space on the beach which again came with an unbelievably low price. We named our place 'Vibe Tribe.' Our little home and restaurant at the beach.

Manifesting healing ~

I was on a beach one evening relaxing with my friend, watching the sunset; a common friend called me up in an emergency, saying his mom had gotten hospitalized for kidney failure and the doctors had given up on her surviving any longer, and she was in a critical condition. His voice stumbled as he requested me to do something, as he knew my ability to manifest anything. I told him not to worry and that his mother will be discharged and be at home in just ten days and disconnected his call. I closed my eyes then, sat on the warm beach sand and tuned into the present moment to lock the potential of his mother's recovery. After I realized I had tapped into the present, I created a thought, a visualization where I was at my friend's place chilling on his couch and watching his mother walk around in the house being healed and feeling grateful to experience this moment in the present moment as if it already happened. I released a huge impulse of electromagnetic energy (feeling) from my heart then, after a few minutes of cherishing that high energy with gratitude, I opened my eyes.

After three days, my friend called me up, saying his mother had now been shifted from the intensive care unit to a normal hospital ward and was recovering at a pace not expected by doctors. After I reached my home town in a week, I went down to the hospital to visit my friend and his mother, and I felt more grateful. After three more days, she got discharged from the hospital, and eventually, my friend invited me down to his place. As I went to his house and chilled on his couch, I saw his mother walking around the house, healthy and healed. My friend then asked me what I had done to heal his mother, and you know what my answer was.

Manifesting the hurricanes to glide away ~

As our restaurant setup was on full force, one cloudy morning, I woke up at the beach hearing a group of people talk to each other with a great amount of stress in their voices and felt like some danger and uneasiness in the air. I got up, went to the bathroom to freshen up, and I felt the wind blowing fast in an unusual way with all the pine trees swinging in full motion. I got out of the bathroom and walked straight to the beach to know what exactly was happening. A few of my restaurant staff were standing near the shore, and I approached them to ask what is the hush about. One of the staff replied, saying there have been hurricanes in the sea since yesterday night, which have wiped off beach shacks in the north of Goa, killing several hundred people and fishermen, and the hurricanes are moving towards south Goa and have caused enough damage to nearby beaches too. Hearing this, I pulled out my phone and called up my friend who was staying at our house a little far from the beach (from the house, we could see the sea, but not the beach shore). His voice also carried a certain amount of fear as he asked me to come over to see him for something important. I picked up my car keys and drove to our second home, where he stayed that night. As I reached, he received me, and we went straight onto the terrace to get a clear view of the sea and its horizon. The winds got heavier to the point that my friend could barely stand without holding on to something. It then started to rain in an unusual way, like big droplets of rainwater flying right and left in an incoherent way. Then my friend pointed out countless medium-sized hurricanes coming closer to the shore; I started to build fear towards what we were experiencing at that moment. My friend, with a certain amount of fear and also confidence in his voice, told me and reminded me about the story I had shared with him that I heard in the Gregg Braden seminar, about the Native American neighbour David, and my mind immediately related to the words of that forty-year old European woman in my meditation when I was in the Himalayas, that I hold power to harness these forces of nature like water and air. My mind convinced me at the moment to put the forty-year-old woman's words into action, or else I would end up with all my investments being washed away by the hurricanes if not me. I realized I didn't have much time and options at the moment anyways, so I sat down on the terrace under a small roof with my legs folded and eyes closed. I told my friend to relax and keep an eye on the hurricanes.

As I sat with my eyes closed, I stopped judging the hurricanes to be good or bad, I stopped building fear against it consciously, and I created energy in my heart feeling how I would feel watching those hurricanes just move away from the seashore and pass on and the feeling of going back to the restaurant and seeing everything in absolute place and all the staff reporting a miracle of the hurricanes missing our beach line magically. I visualized every staff's face; I felt that peace in the air after the storm was over and gave thanks for all of it as if it already happened. As I had lost the trace of time during my meditation, my friend confirmed I had been sitting with my eyes closed for more than thirty minutes, and he saw the hurricanes come close to shore and glide towards the right without touching absolutely anything on our beach. As my friend and I drove down to our restaurant, we were greeted by our staff, and one of them, whom I had seen in my visualization, stepped up to me, saying how the hurricanes drifted away, just leaving a massive power cut because of the winds. The air once again felt calm and felt like a beautiful cloudy evening at the beach. The next day we got reports about the other beach shores, just before and after our beach, got their beach beds, tables, and chairs washed away and leaving them with great expenses and time to repair the damages. I am certain up to this point in this book, most of the stories up here sound more like fiction or fables, but hold on, as you proceed towards the second part of the book, you unveil the science behind some miracles that nature manifests through you, and you will sense the thin line between human and superhuman.

Manifesting an event as desired ~

After a few days of starting and running my restaurant, one evening, I was working at my cash counter, and I saw a pretty, white and chubby girl from England walk into my restaurant with stress wrapped all around her aura. As she took a seat on one of our cocktail chairs, a voice in me asked me to walk towards her and ask her if she is doing fine. When I greeted her and asked her if her day was good, she broke into tears expressing how messed up things got after she got here. This specific beach where I was had countless yoga teacher training academies, and this young woman had come here for a two-month training course. On her arrival at her academy, she faced many issues with her accommodation and cleanliness, and the lead trainer she was here for had to leave on an emergency break. I sat in front of her on the fine bamboo table and chairs we had and asked her to close her eyes and relax her body from head to toe while taking deep breaths and as I sensed she hit a hypnotic state, I made her visualize walking into the training centre and feeling everything in its divine place and getting the best hotel room view and the cleanest. I also guided her to visualize her favourite trainer conducting her sessions and everything going exactly as she desired. With the 60bpm reggae music playing in the background at my restaurant, this beautiful woman experienced a moment of meditativeness, and I asked her to open her eyes after twenty minutes and played her favourite music track on the restaurant music speakers. She left after dining with us that night, and after a week, she came back with a big group of friends from her yoga training academy. As she walked in, she came running towards me, giving me a hug full of gratitude and started expressing how her last week had been. She said, "As I reached the hotel, the receptionist offered her a room that just got vacant, luckily and had the best view of the beach." As she woke up the next morning, her favourite trainer had informed her colleague that he was returning the very next day to start his classes. She mentioned saying, "It felt like magic seeing things conspire in her favour just as she returned to the hotel." She asked in a hilarious tone if I was a witch. I smiled at her, saying, "She is the one in her case," as she is the one who tapped into the infinite potential of her subconscious mind and created the magic in her heart to manifest what she desired, not from a place of lack, and not from a place of judging the unfair and not from a place of feeling victimized, she could feel what she desired, and the universe answered her prayer.

Saving a business from shut down and manifesting 2 million in 2 weeks ~

After working and vacationing on the beach for a season, I returned to my home town to spend time with my family. After a few months, covid started climbing its peak, and the lockdowns were initiated. This happened during the phase between the first and second lockdowns in 2020. One late evening a friend called me up, expressing his business losses and stress about reviving his company or he would be running into a shutdown soon. I asked him what would be the amount of money he would need to fix the losses in his company. He replied in a low and sad note, "Two million Indian rupees!" I requested a day's time to design him a personalized meditation for manifesting two million in no time. I asked him if he had to make two million in his real estate business and how many properties his company would have to sell, and he replied, saying four. I then intervened about his belief about the possibility of making two million in no time and installed a belief that said making two million is easy and very well possible. In his personalized meditation, I guided him into the present moment and made him visualize the below,

"He is seated in his office in his cabin during a pleasant morning, hearing the birds chirp and then hearing his phone ringing from an unknown number. He answers the call and notices an old man calling for an enquiry, and he invites the gentleman down to his office to share prospects. He comes down to the office and agrees to go down for a site visit with my friend's office staff. After visiting the property sites, his client came to his office with a big smile, said he had four children and decided to buy four different properties for each child. He loved the property site and wanted to close the deal. With a big smile on my friend's face, he humbly finishes with the documentation and bids goodbye to his new client with a warm handshake, and the next day he receives a check for two million in his company account for his services. Then I guided him towards feeling grateful and joyful as if it has already happened and the two million is already in his bank account, and his business stabilized." As he had no other choice but to dedicate his morning and night routine to his personalized meditation, he religiously meditated for what he wanted for slightly more than two weeks, and one day as he was sitting in his office, he got a call from an unknown number for an enquiry about the property my friend's company was selling. My friend was not even aware that his brother had placed a newspaper ad for the weekend, and as the gentleman came down to my friend's office, he mentioned he has four sons and likes to buy four different properties around the same site. As my friend's client reached his office, he purchased four properties giving his company a profit of 2 million INR. My friend, in a state of sweet shock, asks me how did all this happen with such accuracy? And I replied, well, it was a prayer well answered!

Manifesting a peaceful end of a conflict and inheritance worth 40 million overnight ~

Just a few days before I started writing this book, I had a client who enrolled on one of my programs; she had contacted me out of desperation after things in her life went haywire. She mentioned the immense stress and anxiety she had been under in the last four months after her father passed away. She and her family had been in a dispute against the will of the father, and she realized she would be losing all her inheritance to her brother, as he had gone far enough manipulating the father's will. I asked her to connect on a Zoom call, and I intervened in her situation and changed her perspective about looking at her present turmoil. After the intervention, I asked her to close her eyes and guided her into the present moment, and made her visualize a peaceful end to this conflict with her brother and others who supported him. I made her feel deeply as if things have already conspired in her favour, and the brother, out of guilt, has respectfully given her share as per the original will. I made her visualize shaking hands with her sister and hugging them out of joy and gratitude for finally receiving their share. The next day she connects with me on a video call, saying it is very important, and she blows up in joy and excitement, expressing how things just flipped overnight and how the brother was effortlessly made to confess his crime of manipulating the father's will. She then asked me what happened differently that made way towards manifesting a peaceful end and an amount of forty million Indian rupees. I then told her it is the shift in perspective towards the whole situation, successfully tapping into the present moment and vibrating what you desire and deserve.

Many times, when we are in a turmoil of misery for too long, our brain gets deeply wired in negative ways, constantly triggering emotions of hatred, anger, envy and pain. Once these emotions get hard-wired in us, it becomes very difficult for us to look at anything in life from a positive mind frame. This low vibrational emotional energy will never manifest anything on a higher plane. That is why forgiveness is the biggest key to releasing all of these negative emotional patterns from our subconscious mind. Once this client forgave her brother in a hypnotic state, she opened doors to what she deserved, and that took just overnight to manifest once she vibrated at the peaceful end of the conflict.

———◆———

Forgiveness is a Super Power

"True Forgiveness is wishing the best for someone who has harmed you."

A client came to me in 2018, expressing her trauma, revenge, helplessness and envy towards her aunt, who has made her go through hell in the process of manipulating property documents and writing everything in her name. Although this stressful phase of my client's life continued for more than a month, she won the legal case eventually, while she had to pay a big check to get her property back. After this incident, she held heavy emotional baggage in her body, boiling up with all the negative emotions every day, witnessing how wonderful the aunt was living her life. Looking at the cycles of misery this sweet client was entangled with for close to two years, I ran an emotional healing therapy on her, helping her forgive their aunt and release the heavy baggage she was holding on. Once she felt light and relieved from this burden after forgiving her aunt from the core of her emotional body, she asked me this question innocently, why do people who cause suffering to others live a far better life than the ones who suffered? How is it fair if God cannot settle something so evident? I smiled and said, darling, today you have removed the biggest blockage of your life by forgiving someone who has harmed you while trusting in God that your forgiveness will not go in vain, and not far in future, you will come back to me telling how God and karma paid back your aunt her share of pain that she put into this world. Forgiveness, on the other hand, is not wishing the worst for the other; this cannot be a high vibrational energy to manifest anything good and deserving for yourself; forgiving someone while wishing the best for the other is when you release the wheel of karma for the other, as pain is what will eventually bring the other wisdom and realization. In 2019 this client got a call from her mother saying the aunt lost her husband in a motorbike accident, and in 2020, the aunt lost her eldest son to an incurable illness. I felt a little sad about the loss of lives, but then I realized this was the divine plan!

After years of my transformation, the vision I got in the Himalayas in one of my meditations about the European woman still haunted me to curiosity about how the five elements of nature are connected to me and what defines this connection. With the heightened sense of awareness I gained, one day, I understood how deep of an empathic connection I have developed for all the five elements, and that is one of the shifts that happened within me during the initial phase of my transformation.

What are the five Elements, and how are they relevant to our lives?

The five elements as we learnt earlier-

Water, Fire, Air, Earth and Ether ~

Everything in the physical world is composed of these five elements. For the physicality to manifest, it requires the assistance and memory of these five elements as the human mind hosts a specific bank of memory called the elemental memory, which decides to formulate the atomic and cellular structure of your body when you are in your mother's womb as an egg. If this memory did not exist in your mental body, then your body wouldn't have taken its shape in the womb. These five elements are the basic building blocks of life itself.

The human body is made up of these five elements too. It is majorly water that is 72% and 12% air, 6% earth, 4% fire, and the rest is ether. Likewise, a rock could be more earth, a bit of fire, a little water and so on. There are various different forms of meditation and breathing techniques to awaken the full potential of these five elements, and they are taught in many different schools of spirituality.

How does one know they have formed a conscious connection to these elements?

When you gain an emphatic connection to these elements, you know that these elements are working in absolute favour with your existence in this universe.

The first thing you will notice in yourself when you align with the **element of water** is that you will start to feel a deep connection with every drop of water you encounter on your skin. When you gain that empathy, respect and connection to this element all around you, your heart will not let you waste a single drop of water. When you bathe, you will feel the water you pour on your body, communicating with the water in your body. Your bathing experience will turn into more of a spiritual cleansing experience than merely just washing the dirt off your physical body. You will connect to the depth of the water element, and you will know it is also responsible for healing your physical nature. You bow down to this element as if it is divine, you drink every drop of water like medicine, and then this element actually starts to behave like medicine, not only for your physical body but also for your mental and spiritual body. You will feel a strong connection between your mind, body and spirit when you connect to the element of water. There have been countless experiments done to express the connection between the physical and the non-physical. The science of cymatics is a wonderful example of the connection between water and our mind (I will discuss the science of cymatics later in this book). So it is clear to understand if you gain balance with this one element in your life, you gain 72% balance in your life.

When you gain the same connection with the **air element**, you will become conscious of every breath you take in and every breath you take out. You will breathe every breath like you are inhaling life; you will find a special connection with trees that give you the purest form of this element. You will know that this element is one of the most powerful keys to accessing higher dimensions of life, which are beyond the ideas of survival. You will know every bit of this element keeps you alive. You will cherish every breath you inhale and exhale. You will know how this element purifies your entire being; you will figure out that it is indeed the most powerful form of drug ever present on this planet. When this happens from the depth of your being, you will know it is an expression of the divine. Connecting with this element will make you empathic towards anything that breathes it in this vast existence. There is huge scientific significance in the relation between our breath and our thoughts. The right way of breathing connects your physical, mental and spiritual worlds in harmony.

When you gain a connection with the **earth element**, every step you place on this planet becomes sacred; everything physical that you touch will display the depth of intimacy towards it. Grounding in nature will become your utmost importance. Walking barefoot will be your most cherished experience. The mountains, the sea, the plants, the soil, and the mud will start beating in your heart. You know that surrendering to this element makes you feel whole and complete. You will know that this element is responsible for your entire well-being. In Japan, forest therapies are some of the most powerful therapies prescribed by authorities of medical sciences to heal your mind, body and spirit.

Fire, when you connect to this element; you will no longer fear the heat this element carries. You will never look at the fire as you have always perceived it. You know, absorbing this element beyond its physical nature is one of the most soothing experiences for your well-being. You will love to stare into the fire and surrender to its light as if it is you. Fire will not seem like any harmful experience. You will know the element of fire ignites the highest potential of your consciousness and increases the zest of achieving all your burning desires, and your success will become a cakewalk. You will bow down to it like divine again. In fact, you will crave the very presence of this element around you as the sun goes down. Your human nature will start to ignite in ways you have never imagined.

The ether has no specific percentage of composition, that's why we can't really say it is the remaining six per cent after water, earth, fire and earth. In fact, it is limitless by its nature. In the human body, this element is one of the most vital as it holds importance that goes well beyond lifetimes. Enhancing this element will connect you to worlds beyond your physical nature; you will notice your intuitive and psychic abilities suddenly rise. You will know that this element holds all the other four elements with harmony and balance. You will become more meditative than ever before. You will eventually feel "connected and one with God" itself. You will feel the true essence of your existence. You will begin to sense the presence of all the major energy centres in your body. You will feel how these energy centres in your body radiate powerful energies, which, if directed to any other living being, can heal the worst of illnesses in them; it can trigger a spiritual awakening in anyone you come close to.

Ultimately when you surrender to every bit of the creation of the divine with love, you know you have gained harmony with these five elements, and every thought you create in your head has no other way but to materialize.

Irrespective of all these events that happened in my life in divine order, it confirmed the superhuman potential in me that had been awakened after experiencing great misery. I still stayed up late at night, wondering what had actually caused this shift in my body and mind before I went to the Himalayas. It constantly kept me on a quest to know the deeper truths of my transformation. It became more important not only to feed my curiosity but make me release; if I can unleash these superhuman potentials in me experiencing misery, I can help people experience this shift without any misery. I understood that only if I could outline what shifted in my biology, I can create the same transformation in others without them brushing through the deepest of their pains.

It took years to hear these voices guiding me closer to truth, and one day I came across the work of another quantum physicist and scientist, Dr Joe Dispenza, a New York Times bestselling author, and my mind comprehended what had happened to me that very night, what shifted in my biology. It was what all the wise ones spoke about, the darkest night of my soul. I can guarantee if you have heard about this phrase, you surely might have tasted a bit of what I am going to express further. The phrase "dark night of the soul" is often mentioned more in the philosophical or mystical arena but brought great understanding to me in the scientific world. The work of this scientist and Sir Gregg Braden and Dr Bruce Lipton (a cellular biologist and master in the field of epigenetics) helped me connect the dots to my experiences and fully comprehend the biological shift during my journey from human to superhuman.

The darkest night of your life will untie the material ribbon of your soul and help you embrace your spiritual nature.

~ **Arf.**

Dark Night of Your Soul

As the saints, sages and mystics have said, the dark night of the soul appears to be the most dreadful experience of one's life, but more than often, the ones who survive it receive a gift, a gift of wisdom and knowledge. My deep curiosity pointed towards the most mystical gland in the human body, a gland that is not discussed much in the medical community as the depth of importance it holds. As I began looking into the biology of this one gland from the eyes of quantum physicists and cellular biologists, it did not surprise me that it hosts a few biological properties similar to the physical eyes. As Dr Joe Dispenza says, "This gland, when tweaked and stimulated in a specific way, creates some of the most powerful elixirs known to mankind".

The pineal gland has long been known to be a mystical gland and clearly defined superhuman abilities. It has held huge significance in every civilization that ever perished on this planet. From Egyptian civilization to the Vedic drooled over this gland as the basis of superiority to human intelligence.

As modern science has come to terms with this mystical gland and its functions in the recent past, it states that this gland is a transducer, a gland which most refers to as the third eye. The new age science has surrendered to an understanding that the pineal gland is the human antenna. It has the ability to transduce the unseen spectrum of light into imagery in our minds. Dr Joe Dispenza says, "the same way a TV picks up frequencies and turns them into pictures on the screen, the pineal gland chemically transduces higher frequencies of electromagnetic energies into vivid, surreal images in the human mind".

The pineal gland turns almost dormant after a certain age while we are growing up due to the heavy socioeducational conditioning we go through and due to the consumption of chemically processed food, and it needs to be activated using certain breathing patterns and techniques. These breathing patterns are taught in some powerful meditations to awaken higher levels of perception and consciousness. A pattern of breathing we breathe while we are crying intensely, a pattern where we pull in a long breath, hold the breath tight, and release with pressure as we exhale. Making this breathing pattern happen in repetition triggers the pineal gland to release some very powerful chemicals in the human brain. These chemicals released in the pineal gland make us experience life in a superhuman way.

Let's look at the biology and function of the pineal gland briefly and see what happens when this [intense crying] specific pattern of breathing is initiated. Generally, the pineal gland produces two main important chemicals in our brain to control our sleep cycles; they are Serotonin & Melatonin.

Serotonin is a chemical responsible for keeping us active and analytical during the day, whereas melatonin is a chemical that's produced when the sun goes down, and it prepares the body for a dream state or sleep.

When melatonin levels rise in our body after sunset, we drift into a semi-dream state, and then when we initiate that specific breathing pattern, as mentioned before, it creates a piezoelectric effect in the pineal gland, compressing and expanding the calcite crystals in it, during the part we hold our breath and squeeze our face muscles and release, we create a powerful electromagnetic impulse into the invisible field of light that hosts infinite intelligence.

When this process takes place in the human mind in a repetitive mode, it gives melatonin an upgrade, and it produces some of the most powerful chemicals known to mankind, which are,

Dimethyl Tryptamine (DMT) – This is a very powerful Hallucinogenic chemical, it is a chemical that makes you see beyond the third-dimensional reality and gives you a peak into the spiritual world, and it will make you lose the sense of space and time. It's the active ingredient to the drink Ayahuasca, used for sacred ceremonies and rituals by the indigenous tribes of Shamans in the Amazon forests. When this chemical is produced in the human brain, we perceive beyond the physical reality. This chemical is technically responsible for making one taste the ability of a multidimensional self. Your ability to see things beforehand, the ability to intuitively dream powerful messages, the ability to tap into the spiritual realms etc., are some of the many multidimensional experiences you encounter when the pineal gland is successfully tweaked to upgrade melatonin into DMT.

Methoxylated indoleamine – This is a phosphorescent bioluminescent chemical in electric eels that amplifies energy in the nervous system. Just imagine how an electric eel gets lit up with energy when stimulated. That's what happens to the brain when this chemical is released by the pineal gland. You might have seen in religious pictures of saints and sages having a hallow light in a circle around their heads. This light illuminates in a way that does not meet the normal eyes but the eyes of people who have a heightened perception. From a normal point of perception, too, it does not go unnoticed, you might have crossed a stranger with a humble smile on a random street, and that grabbed your attention from morning to night, wondering how that stranger was lit up and how well your entire day was after that and you say to yourself, ah what a glow that person had on his or her face.

Tetrahydro-beta-carboline (**Pinolines**) – A very powerful Antioxidant. These pinolines attack the free radicals which harm our cells and cause us to age. These antioxidants are anti-cancer, anti-ageing, anti-heart disease, anti-stroke, anti-neurodegenerative, anti-inflammatory and anti-microbial. When this chemical is released from the pineal gland, your body heals in the most magical ways; the stubborn fat around your belly will melt, the acne on your skin will disappear, and the very structure of your body will take its best shape.

Benzodiazepine – This chemical is a sedative. It is a chemical used in making Valium, "the sleeping pill," it anaesthetizes the analytical mind, so the brain relaxes and stops analysing everything in the outer world. When this chemical is secreted from your pineal gland, the quality of your sleep will enhance, and every night's sleep will make you feel more rejuvenated than ever before.

Methozytrptamine – This is the same chemical that helps some animals hibernate and extend rest and repair their bodies even further. You might have heard stories about mystics, saints and sages getting into meditative states for days or months or even years on end. Yes, this is what Methozytrptamine is responsible for when released in deep states of meditation.

These are the different metabolites of melatonin that are produced when this mystical chemical gets a biological upgrade and the pineal gland tunes into frequencies faster than normal visible light.

To produce these most powerful chemicals in our brains, we have found several different ways to breathe, meditate and tune into higher frequencies of light throughout history in every civilization.

But who knew the universe or the divine had its way of throwing me down by my face and making me experience deep misery and pain and making me cry for days on end till my pineal gland got an automatic upgrade due to that one specific breathing pattern I initiated unknowingly while crying, I start seeing a world beyond the spectrum of light my physical eyes could capture.

As I received this gift after conquering immense pain and misery, my heart ached to find the answers to my ultimate transformation, not only to feed my curiosity but to help others receive their gifts without walking on this harsh path of suicidal trauma. Looking at so many people with my heightened sense of perception was more painful than pleasure, as my empathic heart could sense how everyone was suffering in their psychological misery. I saw each person, from poor to rich, so-called good-looking ones to the ones who think they are not, to people who are healthy to the people who are ill, from a child to an adult to the ones in their old age, I saw every one silently suffering their minds and their capabilities, and on the other side my empathy towards the other also made me see the superhuman in everybody, that just needs to be embraced and that just needs to be awakened!

After almost four years of intensive scientific research and search for the ultimate truth to my magical transformation, to the wisdom I gathered from the Sufis, Yogis and Monks in the high lines of the Himalayas during my sabbatical phase, I designed two of the most powerful training programs, called "embrace the superhuman" and "awaken the superhuman" to help everyone walking on the same journey I once ventured upon, and to help every person I meet unleash their highest potential and live a life that they desire and deserve. This book goes in-depth on "Embrace the superhuman," which will help you understand the finer aspects of healing your mind, to knowledge and wisdom gathered from the work of renowned scientists, mystics and philosophers.

What Qualifies as a Superhuman?

When we hear the phrase "superhuman," we often picture superheroes from Superman and Batman comics or characters from the Avengers movie flying around in capes fighting for justice, and sadly it has confused the real idea of what defines superhuman and putting the whole idea of human evolution in a box of fictional entertainment. The individuals that quantum scientists like Gregg Braden, Dr Joe Dispenza and Dr Bruce Lipton talk about in their series of books like Divine Matrix, Becoming Supernatural, Biology of Belief, You are the Placebo, The Gods Code, Human by Design, Breaking the Habit of Being Yourself, Evolve Your Brain and more, are individuals like you and me, in fact, most of their books have swept their way into mainstream education arena and is a part of standard course curriculum in esteemed institutions like Princeton, Stanford and Harvard. It is clear to see how normal people are doing the superhuman, and these common people have accomplished incredible feats, such as finding happiness while battling a terrible illness or making three-point baskets in basketball to a woman lifting a crashed car in order to save a life to the longest fire pit walk by a normal woman named Amanda Denison that entered the Guinness book of world records.

So, the question arises, is superhuman only limited to our physicality? Or it goes beyond? A famous example is the American Jew, human rights activist and author **Nathan Sharansky**. When Nathan travelled to Russia for official work in the 1970s, he was arrested by the Russian authorities assuming him to be an American spy and was put behind bars for nine long years in a prison cell 3ft by 4ft in size. Nathan realized if he had to get out of prison fit and healthy, he had to keep his mind and body in regular action.

He decided to subject his body to antigravity exercises (using only his body weight) and subject his mind to something positive and rewarding in nature so that the mind and body stay fit and healthy. Along with the antigravity exercises, he decided to play chess with than chess world champion "Gary Kasparov," defeating him every day on that chess board in his mind. For nine years, he continued his exercise until he was released from prison, fit and mentally healthy.

After his release from prison, he travelled back to Israel and joined the cabinet ministry, and one day came, Gary Kasparov to Israel for a demonstration match. A demonstration match is played against multiple opponents to demonstrate one's ability to be a champion. That day Gary had five opponents; he won against four but lost to one. The one he lost to was Nathan Sharansky, and that created a wave of news in the Israeli ministry and media. Nathan was interviewed and questioned how he managed to defeat the world champion when he was not a professional chess player. His response to the media was astonishing. He said, "I played chess with Gary and defeated him 9 into 365 times in my mind, and my mind got programmed to defeat him," that is the key to his victory in that game.

Another such example is **Jack Nicklaus, the number one golfer in American golf history**. When he was asked the secret to his success in being the best golfer, he said I would never hit the ball without properly visualizing the shot all the way into the pothole. He knew if the conscious mind had to control the muscular-skeletal system of the body, it would be an impossible task. But if the subconscious can come into play, it will know how to take the strike. He describes something like this in one of his interviews, "when I hold my golf stick in my hand with the ball on the ground, ready to take a shot, I visualize a perfect swing of my golf stick smoothly lifting the ball of the ground and flying exactly to the spot it has to land and visualize the ball rolling into the golf pot after my mind has comprehended the shot and the score I take a shot almost as relaxed as I am the spectator and the subconscious mind does the rest" and this was his key to becoming the best golfer in American history.

John F Murray, a sport psychologist, former tennis professional and author of the book "Smart Tennis: How to Play and Win the mental game" & the book "Mental Performance Index" has coached many Olympic champions and is famous internationally for his approach to sports performance. In an interview, he says, "When you have to serve the ball in a game like a tennis, first visualize the tossed ball in flight in the court and hold the image of which corner of the court you want the ball to land and then take the shot". The secret behind every successful sportsperson is the power of visualization they have in their mind regarding the sport they play. He had successfully coached Olympic champions and famous tennis and football players and was the most quoted sports psychologist in sports media for a period of two decades.

Norman Cousins, author of the book "Anatomy of the Illness" was diagnosed with a serious collagen illness, a disease of connective tissue; all arthritic and rheumatic diseases fall under this category. Collagen is a fibrous substance that holds all the cells together; in simple words, his body was on a major breakdown heading straight into the grave as his spine began to disintegrate. After trying various different types of pharmaceutical treatments and witnessing no development in his health, he decided to tap into the power of his mind to heal his grave illness. He said he would just use the power of his mind to heal the body. He describes his core work towards healing as humour, belief and courage. What Norman did was, drive down to the nearby movie cassette store and buy several of his favourite comedy movies, and watch them endlessly, laughing his gut out, and he would visualize his vibrant health every day and feel how it would feel with a healthy body totally free from this disease. He also realized the fact that vitamin C is not produced in the human body but only received from the outer side and is the best for boosting immunity. After consulting his doctor friend, he took high doses of ascorbic acid through intravenous drips. In just a period of a few months, he was diagnosed that he was free from an irreversible illness, and he continued to live for another twenty years. Was it the humour in the comedy movies that healed him? Or the belief that he had already healed? Or the courage to ingest excessively high doses of ascorbic acid? Yes, it was all three demonstrating the power of the human mind.

Well, these are just a few such examples of the mind doing the superhuman when it gets trained in specific ways.

When discussing remarkable people, the question of whether they are products of nature or nurture—genes or environment—is frequently raised.

Dr Bruce Lipton says, "Your environment affects the expression of any genes you have irrespective of the genetic disposition," expressing the new science of Epigenetics. This new age science clearly proves that the expression of genes can be under our choice if one gains conscious control over their mind. The new age science of "Mind Over Matter" is capable of releasing the crux of misery from the lives of billions as we now know that we are not slaves to our "genetic disposition" or even our "environment" as the mind is well capable of transcending both the genetic and epigenetic consequences and create what it desires from your genetic level.

So, you are able to achieve greatness in anything if you work at it by being conscious and dedicated enough with the needed belief in yourself? That's a sweet thought, and as sweet as it sounds, it is also real as modern-age science recently revealed the power of the human mind and body from its quantum level and how it influences our lives.

Why is the human race the most superior race?

We have recorded our uniqueness since we first learned to write. Over 2,000 years ago, the philosopher Aristotle outlined our distinctions. As "rational animals," we are interested in learning for its own sake. He said, "We live by art and reason."

"We are genetically very similar; that much is certain. You and a banana are 60% the same genetically; you and a monkey share 98% of the same genes.

The analogy of how much better birds, animals, and other species are than us is endless; some birds fly as fast as our single-engine Cessna aeroplanes, some animals run way faster than us, and some can even reproduce without the opposite gender's involvement, so what is it that makes us different from every other specie in the animal kingdom, it's not just the capability to use verbal and nonverbal language or read and write?

The answer is the mind. The human mind is capable of hosting two faculties that make us stand poles apart in terms of our abilities when we operate at our optimum. The first faculty is the powerful memory we host, and the second is the powerful sense of imagination, which is indeed a super power as it gives the human race an edge to be closer to the divine creator and have the capability to craft one's life from a conscious will. When we train our mind to consciously imagine and visualize using the fragments of memory we have, in combination with a high vibrational feeling, it is what puts us way above the league of any superior animal.

Well, the sad part is this, the two most powerful faculties we have that are supposed to make us the most superior specie on this planet has turned against most of us and is now our enemy, so it is not wrong to say a lot of other animal species are living a life far more joyful than us. The crux of this book is about just this, to help ignite the highest potential of an individual by gaining conscious control over these two faculties and help you create a life that you desire and deserve.

Instead of using your memory bank to downregulate your emotional states, you can rather use your memory bank to imagine, feel and create what you desire.

We most certainly owe the fact that we are superior to every specie on this planet, even being genetically and biologically very much the same.

Chapter - 2

Conscious Mind and The Subconscious Mind

What is the conscious mind and the subconscious mind?

Contemporary western sciences often see the mind as two parts, conscious and subconscious. The subconscious mind is the unit which stores all the memories and neurological patterns dedicated to every action, emotion and belief and also an infinite source of intelligence called intuition (which is mostly dormant). The act of you getting up every day from bed and going to the bathroom and grabbing your toothbrush and applying toothpaste on it and brushing in only a specific manner is the performance of the subconscious mind, or if you are driving on a high way and another driver cuts you off, your subconscious response to it will be probably yelling at the top of your voice with the windows rolled up. But if you are a conscious being, a being that attained a meditative mind, your conscious mind says, let him go! You can choose to be happy and not pay any energy to this unnecessary event. Sadly, the percentage of the memory based subconscious mind we use on a regular basis is

95%, which is why healing the subconscious mind is of utmost importance.

The conscious mind is like the security guard at the main gate. This is the door way of rational analogy and decision-making towards accepting anything into your subconscious mind. The conscious mind works on two operating systems, one is duality, and the other is the polarity (though the concept of duality and polarity exists in many frames of sciences, this is my personal understanding of the conscious mind's operating systems). The duality state of the conscious mind works with the first three departments of the subconscious mind (we will look deeper into the subconscious mind on the next page), which is used for comparative and judgemental analogy; it can only perceive the outer environment in regards to comparing two events stored in the memory bank of the subconscious mind, or comparing the event happening outside of themselves at the moment with another similar event that happened in the past, this is called duality or a dual state of consciousness.

The polarity consciousness works with the fourth department of the subconscious mind, the intuitive mind. Analysis from this state of consciousness happens without comparison, judgement, or distinguishing factors. Since this state of consciousness is untouched by memory, it hosts infinite intelligence. From the polar state of consciousness, you will simply know the analysis without any calculations, or you will consciously choose to use the memory if needed and not compulsively get entangled with multiple thoughts.

Sadly, duality consciousness is the standard operating system that we are programmed with since we are born, hence reducing intuitive intelligence to the bare minimum. Understanding this, it will not be wrong to say, polarity consciousness works more on the emotion of love (as it is a conscious choice), and duality works more using the emotion of fear and is a compulsive choice. Duality consciousness needs no awareness; it's an auto pilot program only for survival and safety; polarity consciousness needs awareness to function; it is a deep state of simply knowing. Let's look at a basic example of both these operating systems; if I am someone who operates on duality consciousness and I am driving my car to work, I will take a left or a right, comparing what happened the last time I had taken this route and take the decision based on this past, present comparative analysis. If I was someone operating on polarity consciousness and was driving to work, I would take a right when my silent mind prompts me to take a right or left with "love, trust and confidence," and more than often, I will gracefully not meet much traffic or any mishap on that route. This state of decision making happens on divine command, not on the comparison. The very first quote in this book, in fact, the very first piece of wisdom that I had written, I mention exactly this, "*Everything in this universe is interconnected with synchrony, hence giving divine power to the expression of the omnipresent source, giving the sense to comprehend divine wisdom and knowledge. Memory starts to fade away, and knowing begins the play.*"

When you awaken to polarity consciousness or transcend duality, you, as an omnipresent expression of the divine, connect to a realm known as the quantum realm (we will learn about the quantum realm or quantum field ahead in the book in detail), and this realm hosts well synchronised infinite intelligence as compared to the finite memory bank. And when this happens, your memory will barely be of any relevance to your future decisions because "knowing" began its play, and you will simply know what is needed in the present moment and what is not.

The chatter in our mind that is on all day and all night is the noise of the subconscious mind, precisely to be the first three departments that are intellect, identity and memory. This noise plays in cycles of 60-100 thoughts per minute in an average human mind. Although all these thoughts may not be in our awareness, it's easy to understand that we are always vibrating the electromagnetic charge of each such unaware thought. Now I invite you to imagine if the standard emotion of your subconscious mind is fear, then every subconscious thought that is vibrating is by default low in nature, and when our average energy field is low in nature, how will we have space to invite any high vibrational manifestation into our life? Reducing this chatter in one's mind is what points us towards the highest searched word on the internet during the pandemic, that is "meditation". Meditation is a tool used primarily for reducing this unnecessary noise in the mind so that a higher state of consciousness is attained (polarity consciousness) and has been used by every civilization that ever perished on this planet to live a far more fulfilling and successful life. When this chatter in mind reduces to 20–30 thoughts per minute or below is when you will have the capability to choose love over everything your five senses touch and simply be guided by divine knowing.

The Subconscious Mind Explained in Four Different Parts

According to ancient sciences, the human mind has sixteen departments divided into four major divisions. Intellect, Identity, Memory and Intuition are these categories—the four mental faculties that many ancient civilizations thrived on to nurture, balance and develop.

Together, the first three cannot operate without each other. Think of them like a wheel with three spokes. The core (thought) is stationary, while the wheel spins to give us views of our physical reality, like behaviour, habits and perception. The fourth part, intuition, is untouched by the first three.

The intellect

This dimension of the mind is a fairly important one for survival, for defragmenting or dissecting physical life. The intellect is what helps you take decisions based on the memory you have. It is a dissecting tool, a tool that distinguishes between present and memory and based on comparative analogy, it decides what is the best for you. Since this dimension of the mind is considered to be a dissecting tool, it works best when it is sharp. So, a man with sharp intellect can manoeuvre his life better than the other who is less intellectual. The intellect is a good tool to use if it is used purely based on memory. But the problem is our brains are programmed to use intellect with the second part of the mind, which is identity. Say, for example, if you identify yourself with a specific nation, specific caste, religion etc., the duty of your intellect is to protect this identity using its sharp dissecting knife. It is not wrong to protect your identity, but the problem is this razor-sharp knife can go to any extent to preserve its identity even at times when not needed because it is compulsive and repetitive in nature.

The Identity

It is known to be the hand that holds the knife, according to ancient sciences. The identity also loosely translates to the ego. As we know, when we are born, we own a universal identity, but as we grow up in these humanistic societies, we develop a sense of identity of who we individually are; we create a distance between our newly found identity to our ultimate universal identity. As the famous Indian mystic says, it is not bad to use this knife to understand and comprehend physical reality by dissecting it, but to know the ultimate or to know beyond the physical; the identity is what holds us behind. It's like if you need to know the biology of an organ, you surely can use a clinical knife to dissect it and see what lies beneath the skin layer or the tissue layer of the organ etc. But if you have to know the nature of your child, you surely do not want to follow the said process, as this may let you know what is inside your child but not enough to let you know the nature of your child. Dismantling the identity to the bare minimum for the said reasons has been the epitome of many ancient civilizations for achieving their highest potential. Have you realized that when you are in an unknown territory, where your identity is minimum, you naturally become more humble and kind? For example, if you are taking directions from an unknown stranger in an unfamiliar land, you surrender and humble down more than regular naturally.

The Memory

This department of the mind is where you hold memory from the beginning of time. To simplify it a little more, this department of the mind records everything your five senses have experienced since you opened your eyes till today (and much more), however much is beyond our present awareness to capture. This third spoke of your wheel is all it needs to make the first two function to their best or worst. Every calculation your identity does, to every action or decision your intellect takes, is retrieved from this bank of information. However, it is also true that memory holds barely any importance if intellect and identity are dismantled. I am sure you now wonder, what happens when these three spokes of the wheel brake and the point of thought dissolve? The fourth dimension of the mind gets activated and dominant from being dormant.

Intuitive intelligence

This department of the mind is considered to be the highest source of intelligence which is untouched by memory, identity and intellect; technically, you gain access to this dimension of the mind when you transcend the first three. Many saints, sages and mystics have said when you touch this part of your mind, your mind dissolves into the divine, and you access fields of information you have no memory of. To understand this a little deeper, your general knowledge is what your memory hosts and the specialized knowledge are what your intuitive mind hosts. You may wonder what will happen to my life if my identity, intellect and memory dissolve. How will I live my life? It's certain to have these questions line up in your mind, but as said earlier, when you access this dimension of the mind, you will just know what is needed and what is not; you will know what is right or what is wrong, you will know if you have to take a left or a right, your mind is no more taking decisions based on your memories. It's like when you are driving; you would not need any memory or even the GPS; your mind will guide you towards taking a right or a left.

To understand the four departments of mind in a deeper way, the metaphor of our cell phone suits the best.

Cell phones are a metaphor for explaining the mind

As the language of psychology is hugely inspired by the metaphoric dialect, let's look at the human mind as something smarter than us, i.e., our smartphone. Our smartphone, just like all of us, also has a name. Let's call it

Samsung or iPhone. It offers us an x amount of technology to use, and recent statistical research on the technological use of our extended limb barely averages 12 to 13% of its actual potential. However, it helps us more than our hand would have ever helped. Similar research has been done on the optimum capacity of the human brain, and what we actually use is sadly a per cent or two less than our smartphones.

As we are talking about this metaphor, our smartphone hosts a technology called the "memory bank" and an "intellect" called the RAM and "identity" that brands, as our example, Samsung or iPhone, and the internet (WIFI or Data) as "intuitive intelligence." Within these four aspects of the smartphone, we can use a good variety of applications it has to offer. We can scroll our way to any corner of the world without taking a single direction from any stranger, connect with anybody on the other side of this planet in a second, to run our entire million-dollar business online barely with an effort.

Now I would like to invite you to imagine that our smartphones have every facility to offer but not the internet. What services do you think it can offer without this one thing called the Internet? What do you think would be your phone's limitations? How would you navigate without the MAP, or how about no Google search on your phone? Or how about no WhatsApp? Don't worry, though; the front camera still works without the internet. However, in this case, using a smartphone would stand a disgrace not only to the user but also to the phone.

According to science and research human mind receives an input of forty million bytes of information per second, and out of which, we only use 44000 bytes per second due to the limitation our five senses have to offer, which is barely 4%. Where do you think is that missing 96% of information going, and what significance can it hold to our existence and life? In other words, it means we are missing out on the navigation system the human brain has to offer, or we are missing the Google search our brain has to offer, or we are missing on sending those pouted selfies to our loved ones through the WhatsApp or Snapchat of our brain?

Yes, the human brain is as dumb as our smartphone without the internet when not using its optimum facility called intuitive intelligence.

Brain and The Heart Connection

The Powerful connection between the Brain and the Heart.

As we understood in chapter one, the human brain is the most complex mechanism available to mankind to decode all that it is capable of performing. The sophistication of this one organ has been under the limelight of educational arenas for centuries. Every civilization thrives to enhance the capabilities of this one organ that also hosts the two most important glands (the Pineal and Pituitary glands) in the human body, which are majorly responsible for making one experience superhuman.

When we understand that the brain is an organ that is physical in nature, the mind is what is psychological in nature. It will be appropriate to say that the mind is the brain in action. The connection between this hardware and the software is the neural circuitry which is stored in the form of patterns, or some call it programs. Whenever we do or perform a task that is new, we automatically create a pattern of neural connections dedicated only to the newly learnt program. For example, if you have just started to learn how to drive a car, your mind will dedicate one corner to this skill in a complex pattern in the brain. So, when you continue to drive every day, this complex neural connection becomes hardwired to the extent that after a few years, you will drive without thinking about the controls. The same goes for every single task we perform in our daily life. Every task has a place dedicated in our mind to wire and fire those neurons when needed. In fact, the science of many psychotherapies is just this, we disconnect the link between your hardware and the software using linguistics or language, and when the software is uninstalled, the hardware or neural circuitry will eventually dissolve as it has no use anymore.

What is energy and vibration?

Let's look at this hardware that we call the brain and heart in a different way, the brain is more electrical in nature and less magnetic, and the heart is more magnetic and less electric.

As we know, we have equipment in the hospital laboratories that measure the brain/heart's electrical activity using EEG (electroencephalography) and MEG (magnetoencephalography) equipment that measures magnetic field of the brain/heart; it is enough to help one understand that we are "electro-magnetic beings" and all of us have our individually distinctive electromagnetic fields of vibrations. The electromagnetic vibration of a person is what we call energy. The amount and quality of energy we harness every day determines the quality of our life.

As we look closer at the software that is the mind, every thought produced in the mind creates an electromagnetic charge equivalent to the quality of that thought. This electromagnetic charge created by the brain in action triggers a cascade of chemicals to release from all the necessary glands and this complex combination of chemicals released from every gland and meeting at the gut blending with more chemicals that can be termed as an emotion. So, it is appropriate to conclude thoughts are majorly electrical in nature and emotions are chemical, and it is not wrong to say emotions are the premature physical manifestations of thoughts, which in turn make you feel good or bad.

Let's look at emotions a little deeper now; emotions are of only two types, one is Love and the other is fear, though it is expressed by the spiritual communities in a little different way; they say emotion is only one; it is love and the absence of love, which either way draw a line between positive emotions or negative emotions. For the sake of this book, let's look at emotions to be Love and the opposite be fear.

The cascade of chemicals meets after the thought has been infused with either love or fear. For every thought that is produced in our mind, we have a choice, a choice to feed it with the emotion of love or the emotion of fear. The sad part is this choice is available to people who are conscious and aware. As we grow up in our typical societies, we are programmed to choose everything based on the emotion of fear. The emotion of fear is more promising because it promises to keep you safe and in known territories. Technically, being safe is not bad, but what is the meaning of life that has not been experienced with the emotion of love?

Here is a small example to help you understand this a little deeper; imagine you are trekking up a hill to enjoy a beautiful landscape view, and once you reach the top hill, you got mesmerised looking at the view, and you have the option of choosing to infuse this experience with the emotion of love. Still, the distracted and fear-based programmed mind knocks on the door of your gut and says, what if it gets dark before you get down the hill, or what if there are wild animals around waiting for a tasty meal? What if there are thieves with knives hiding somewhere around? Oh yes, you confirm, I saw that on that crime patrol TV show, or that happened to my friend's uncle, and there goes down the drain your chance to cherish the most beautiful landscape up on the hill.

Let's look at the conscious mind and the subconscious mind in reference to the famous "law of attraction" that has impacted the lives of millions around the globe. I refer to the conscious mind as the creator and the subconscious mind to be the chief editor for a reason because the conscious mind is where we can create a thought and then a feeling corresponding to the conscious/subconscious choice of an emotion. As we learnt in the earlier chapters, "feeling is the prayer." The purest form of feeling your heart generates is the purest form of prayer you can ask for, but the catch is this chief editor is preprogramed, and every thought you create has to bypass the decision of this editor. If the editor has an opposite program to what you desire to manifest, then the feeling that you create will be edited automatically from the compulsive emotional frame. For example, if I desire to buy a mansion and my subconscious mind has a program that says I cannot afford a mansion, the feeling that corresponds to the thought will be a very low vibrating impulse that says it is impossible to afford the such expensive luxury, and there goes your conscious desire out of the window as the emotion subconsciously chosen behind this feeling is a branch of fear. Or we could say when you create a conscious thought about having an abundance of wealth, but you have the emotion of fear more dominant, then the feeling you create will be equivalent to "Ah, how can I have an abundance of wealth and finances when I am not worth it, or I don't even have a college degree where would I get this wealth from? Or there are many people who are miles smarter than me. How would I even stand a chance? Or I have been taught that poor or middle-class people have a difficult life and we have no choice but to surrender to these difficulties. What I am trying to say is the chief editor will ultimately use the dominant emotion of fear that translates into envy, jealousy, unlucky, lack, victimized, cursed etc. and retune your thought's electromagnetic field into a lower vibration.

One of the most powerful sources of electromagnetic energy that can be generated on this planet is the energy the human heart generates.

We have all heard this sweet romantic phrase; I will love you to the moon and back, hilariously originates from a scientific understanding that concludes the amount of electromagnetic energy the human heart generates when tuned in to the energy of love and is enough to fuel up a rocket from earth to the moon and back.

Let's look at the heart in a brief comparison with the brain. The heart generates an electrical field that is a hundred times higher than that of the brain and a magnetic field that is five thousand times more powerful than the brain. This piece of science is enough to conclude that the human heart is a very powerful magnet. This also explains how feelings are more magnetic in nature. Quantum sciences today also claim we are electromagnetic beings; even this physical reality we perceive is a band of electromagnetic fields condensed in a low vibrational field of matter. This means when you like to manifest a Lamborghini, using the power of your heart's electromagnetic field, you are actually magnetizing the information stored in the electric charge that carries the thought of you driving a Lamborghini, and not to forget, the so-called Lamborghini supercar is also an electromagnetic field condensed in a low field of matter that can be magnetized if both the poles of creator and creation vibrationally match. So, it is not about the material vibration of the car, which is a low field of condensed energy, but the vibration your heart will feel when you are owning and driving it. If your desire is to manifest a Lamborghini, but your average electromagnetic field only fits in a Toyota (which you already drive, for example), where is the vibrational match to your desire? And where is the possibility of you attracting it into your life when laws of physics fail to apply?

Among the work of many quantum physicists, evolutionary scientists, and biologists stands out the work of these renowned three scientists we spoke about in the earlier chapters of this book, Gregg Braden, Dr Joe Dispenza and Dr Bruce Lipton. Their contribution to this field of science is remarkable, and they have healed and transformed millions of lives worldwide in the past few decades using the science of transcendental meditation. The work of these evolutionary scientists revolves around the intrinsic connection between the brain and the heart. The literature and knowledge they present to the world have been changing the course of science to new and higher potentials. The wisdom poured out through their enormous expeditions into the high line of Tibet and the Himalayas in the 1990s to the research and publications presented behind thousands of brain scans they monitored in regards to this new age science explain only one thing loud and clear, call it the law of attraction or call it the law of magnetism, or simply call it prayers being answered, the key behind all this is a powerful visualization combined with the high emotion of love and in turn generate the most powerful feeling, and as said earlier, "feeling is the prayer".

Letting this sink in can be a slow and gradual process, but the feeling you generate should be out of a visualization that is constructed in the "present tense" and being fully associated (like looking from your own eyes). The reason behind the visualization being in the present tense is that the law of attraction works only when the vibration of your desire and the vibration of your present feeling is of match. Another example is if I like to manifest a new house, the vibration of my prayer or feeling should carry the vibration and feeling I would carry when I stay in my dream house, not the vibration that states I will one day live in my dream house. If your feeling is in the future tense, then all you manifest will be "I will one day" or "I will soon" have a house that I desire.

Many ancient cultures, religions and civilizations had this truth hardwired in their systems, but sadly modern civilization has been far from this powerful truth and understanding.

The power of thought on our brain and body

The Great Experiment by the Harvard Team of Scientists for a Five-Finger Piano Exercise

Volunteers were invited to a lab at Harvard Medical School to learn and perform a simple five-finger piano exercise for two hours a day for five days. The experiment was relatively small. Alvaro Pascual-Leone, a neuroscientist, had this group of volunteers who had never played a piano before. He divided the group into two.

The first group was asked to practice the piano using their fingers like the way a piano is played. The second group of volunteers were asked to practice playing the piano, not using their fingers but playing only in their minds (visualizing it). Both groups were subjected to before and after brain scans after each day of training. Researchers discovered that after only five days of training, the region of the motor cortex in the brain responsible for these finger motions spread like dandelions throughout a suburban field.

The researchers caught a glimmer of a novel concept about the brain when they examined the brain scans (TMS data) from the two groups (those who really played the piano and those who imagined doing so). These brain scans showed that the same area of the brain that controls the fingers while playing the piano also grew micro millimetres in size in the brains of participants who imagined playing the piano.

Later, Pascual-Leone would conclude, "Mental practice resulted in a comparable restructuring of the brain." If his findings are generalizable to other types of motion (and there's no reason to believe they aren't), then it could be possible to improve at golf, football, swimming or at any sport or art by also focusing on the mental aspects of the movements rather than only the physical ones. The finding was even more ground breaking since it demonstrated the ability of mental training to alter the brain's physical structure.

Why is the experiment important to your life?

So, Why does this experiment matter so much? Is it that we can only use this knowledge to outsmart the game of sports or music? Or it holds more relevance to our lives?

A significant and life-changing fact was unearthed by this experiment and the many that have followed. What we consciously experience changes the way our brains are wired. It's not simply what we do to it that changes it; even without moving a muscle, our minds are capable of doing so. It also means as we program our brain beforehand of an experience we desire to manifest, our brain creates neurological patterns in the subconscious mind responsible for that experience we desire, which makes it easier to manifest as "the editor"(the subconscious mind) now is already bribed and will sanction that feeling to pass and manifest what you desire.

This is a glimpse into the interconnected quantum universe we live in. Considering this finding, what do you think its implications are? Does it only validate what we have known for millennia from our many spiritual traditions? In what ways may it affect you? What are your reactions and thoughts?

It will not only introduce you to the power of our Maker in our anatomy but also introduce you to cutting edge research that will revolutionize many aspects of your life in the near future.

The Experiment at Cleveland Clinic: Flexing biceps only by thought

As early as 2004, researchers at Ohio's Cleveland Clinic Foundation investigated the potential health advantages of seeing oneself engage in a strength training program. Their research was titled "Mental Strength: A Path to Physical Strength". Ten young, healthy adults volunteered for this research and were taught techniques for making the directed "imagined" movement (of the fingers and biceps) appear as real as possible in their minds. Muscle strength was assessed before, during, and after the "imagined" training sessions; the researchers saw a 35% boost in finger strength and a 13% boost in bicep strength, significantly large in numerical terms of power! They were recorded to maintain this muscle strength for three months after the study. New motor units inside the muscle and connections with the brain were formed, all of which increased muscular strength.

The researchers came to the conclusion that the mental training techniques used in their study amplify the signal that stimulates the muscles to a greater degree of activation, thereby increasing strength. Do you feel the cohesive connection between these ideas? The results of that study and the many that followed showed that training by mental visualization of powerful muscular contractions was successful in increasing muscle strength without actual physical exercise.

Putting things into context

"Imagination is more essential than science," stated Albert Einstein. As you can see, visualizing the action you want to take is a great way to train your muscles and improve your performance without really doing the work. Mental exercise, if not equally effective as physical exercise, surely holds a great impact on building muscle. Do you think it's possible to live a happy, prosperous life just by deciding to do so? If the best athletes in the world, do it, then I think it's worth giving a try.

How do you think these experiments can relate to your healing?

The story of Nathan Sharansky from chapter one demonstrated the same science. Nathan spent nine long years playing chess in his mind, defeating the than chess world champion nine into 365 times, and thus creating a neurological hardware in his brain that was programmed to defeat the world champion. When the time came, Nathan's mind did what it was programmed to do. This is referred to as priming the mind-body for an experience that you desire to manifest before the actual experience. Also, in the case of America's best golfer, he primes his mind before taking a shot, which means he first creates the necessary hardware and software in his brain for a successful shot and then effortlessly takes the shot.

These experiments not only support the brain circuitry to perform better at sports or any task you like to master and manifest, but it also holds great importance for your healing. Like in the case of Norman's cousins, visualizing a healed version of himself created the necessary programs and neural connections in his brain to manifest himself free from an irreversible disease.

If one is suffering from an illness, a simple mental practice of visualizing a healed self is enough to bring your healing into familiar territory by creating neural networks in your brain as if your healing has already happened. When the time comes, your body will accustom to your healing more effectively and manifest health in the most magical ways. So, it's right to say when the mind perceives your desire to heal in a neurological way, the body follows!

The Science of Cymatics and Water

Cymatics is a field of science that studies sound and vibration and its influence on physical matter. Though there are many scientists who appealed to the scientific communities by presenting their study on the subject of cymatics, Dr Emoto, a Japanese scientist and author of the book "The Hidden Messages in Water" reveals in his study and research that the molecular structure of water is heavily influenced by thoughts, words and emotions. He claims that water is not a passive substance but an intelligent field of information that is alive and responsive in nature. In one of his studies, Emoto took two different jars of water and labelled one to be love and gratitude and the other to be hate and anger. He then took a droplet of water from both the jars and flash-froze them, and examined the molecular structure of both the droplets of water under a microscope.

The water droplet from the jar that was labelled "love and gratitude" displayed beautiful symmetrical and hexagonal crystals, while the water droplet from the jar that was labelled "hate and anger" formed ugly-looking complex crystal structures. He concluded his research as evidence that positive and negative emotions dramatically affect the molecular structure of water.

Another research conducted by a group of students in a university claimed very similar results on plant life. In this study, the students took two plants and labelled one pot with "love" and the other pot with "hate" and placed both plants in two different rooms. All the students in the university were instructed to speak words of love and compassion to the plant that was labelled love and were asked to speak words of hatred to the other plant that was labelled hate every time they entered the rooms where these plants were placed respectively. In a span of a few days, the plant that was labelled love grew healthier and stronger, whereas the plant that was labelled hate deteriorated. Knowing that plants are 90% water, this study revealed how the health of a plant is influenced by human emotion.

Now I invite you to think about what impact negative emotions would have on us, considering the human body is 72% water, and the brain is 90% water. What impact would you leave on another or yourself when your mind is majorly consumed by negative thoughts, emotions and beliefs?

———•———

Chapter - 3

What Is Quantum Science, And How Does It Work?

We could not even imagine a universe that did not contain observers [us] because it is the act of us observing the universe that makes the universe as it is.

~ *Professor John Wheeler, quantum physicist, scientist.*

As a child, when I was eight or ten-year-old, I used to lie down in some corner of my house all alone, thinking about what if I was not born. Where would I be? What would I be? And how real is this experience? How is this life happening? What could be the absence of this life? As a child, I was not satisfied by all the reality checks and teachings delivered to me by my elders. I was taught that this physical life was all to my existence and that after I died, I would be nobody in this physical life leading to an unimaginable torturous afterlife if I didn't live this life according to the norms of religious and societal conditions. This quest to know life had kept me awake long at night, wondering why my existence was of no value to this world and I was just a speck of dust floating around. I would just wave my hand into the emptiness around me and think, why is this empty space so empty, and what is the reason for this emptiness around me? As science taught us growing up, this emptiness is nothing but a place to hover our bodies around, and if something hard hits our toe, it is not empty towards that side. However, as I grew up to be an adult, I believed there is no significance to this emptiness around us, the distance between you and your neighbour, the distance between our planet and the other planet, the distance between our star and the other star, all is just emptiness.

During my phase of transformation, I started experiencing life all over again as a child; all these questions that were left unanswered were surfacing in my mind again, but this time it was with deeper thirst and curiosity. By then, my experience of life had gained a balance between the physical and the nonphysical; I started feeling the emptiness around me in ways which are still difficult to express. Every bit of this experience was pointing towards the emptiness around me, which stretched all around the entire universe. Then one day, as expressed in chapter one, intuitively, I was introduced to the work of some of the most powerful quantum physicists of modern times, whose work is all about the emptiness around us, who have expressed the presence of this emptiness as not emptiness but as a very intelligent field of information. Gregg Braden talks about this field in his book "The Divine Matrix" as a field of information that is beyond our subatomic structure, a field that is just waves and frequencies. Father of Quantum physics, Max Plank, calls this field a matrix and a lot of other scientists explain this field as a quantum field or simply the field. The work of these scientists, who brought a twist into the arena of science, clearly explains our nonstop communication with this emptiness around us.

As John Wheeler said, the act of us looking at something with the expectation of finding something is the act of creation itself; that is why no matter how much we dig into finding the smallest particle of matter, we will always find one more particle smaller than the previous one. Scientists have built big machines, really big machines, to break the smallest piece of matter by accelerating them at a speed close to the speed of light and crashing into each other to break them into smaller pieces of matter. It is a never-ending mission for the scientific community because these experiments conducted on huge cyclotron machines will never find the smallest particle of matter, or like how the scientific communities have been striving to find the edge of the universe, will always create another distance probably towards the edge of the universe itself and finding the edge is out of the question as concluded by the famous quantum physicist.

There have been countless scientific experiments in the past few decades concluding the same, and that brings to our understanding how powerful the human mind is in terms of creation. Now imagine when many of us, who are conditioned to breed in fear, look into our body every day to find some discolouration, some lump, some uneasiness, some disease; then what are we creating for ourselves? What are we manifesting in our bodies by constantly looking for something negative? It is not wrong to take care of your body beforehand, but when we realise, we are powerful creators and every second we are creating our life, then why don't we look at ourselves every day and say, wow, what an amazing body, wow I am becoming healthier and fitter?

QUANTUM FIELD:

What is the quantum field?

As we know, we are skin on our surface, then flesh, then organs, then tissue, then we are cellular, then we are molecular, then we are atomic at ousr physical depth. Beyond our subatomic structure, we are waves and frequencies. These waves and frequencies are all in an infinite band of electromagnetic energy. In fact, as we understood earlier, everything physical that we sense is also a specific band of the electromagnetic energy field, just vibrating at very low and condensed waves and frequencies; perhaps that is why ancient cultures and civilizations called this physical reality an illusion. The nature of waves and frequencies is such that they are always moving, they are coming, and they are going, and all that you desire to manifest in your life already exists in this infinite field of possibilities as waves and frequencies. It is when you tune in to this field as pure awareness and lock these waves and frequencies with a belief of it as if it has already manifested you lock these waves into standing waves, and you trigger the process of your manifestation coming to life at that moment. In this highly intelligent quantum field, the invisible energy field of waves and frequencies of your desired manifestation collapses into a particle, what we call an electron, only when an observer creates a thought on something real and looks for it in this field and locks it as a standing wave using the power of thought and feeling. This is called "collapsing the wave function or a quantum event" in quantum science.

If we have to imagine how this field looks like, imagine shutting off all your five senses, like deactivating your sense to see, hear, feel, touch and taste, then switch off your memory banks, and that is when you enter the void, the eternal blackness or simply waves and frequencies. The quantum field is an invisible field of energy, information, intelligence and collective consciousness that exists outside of our physical nature. There is nothing material or physical there. In the quantum field, the only way to be is as awareness. This intelligent quantum field is also much spoken of in the spiritual communities as the "present moment". We have all heard this popular advice, "Be in the present moment", and this is exactly what it refers to; by being in the present moment of meditativeness or the quantum field, we gain the most powerful ability to be superhuman to be the creator of our own lives.

The Power of Creating A Loop of Thought, Emotion, And Feeling in The Quantum Field

Thought or thinking happens in the brain, emotions happen in the gut, and the feeling happens in the heart. As we already know, thoughts are majorly electrical in nature, emotions are chemical in nature, and feelings are more magnetic in nature. When you create a thought, your brain creates an electrical signal that sends chemicals to the gut, and there these chemicals blend into another complex chemical and are then sent to the heart. The heart then creates a huge electromagnetic field in response to the chemical sent from the gut, called the feeling, and one of the most powerful feelings is belief.

Let's look at thought, emotion and feeling separately. Thought or a visual can be from your memory or intuition, and once created or recalled, the brain creates an electromagnetic charge in line with the nature and quality of your thought. Deeper the detail about the thought you create, the higher the energy impulse, and you lock the desired possibility in the infinite quantum field more effectively.

As we learnt earlier, emotion can only be of two types, that is, love or fear. Love can be broken down into higher emotions like joy, compassion, bliss, happiness, ecstasy, etc., while fear can be broken down into negative emotions like hate, envy, jealousy, competition, resentment, etc. We understood earlier whatever the thought may be; we are programmed to choose either of the two emotions when infused by the electromagnetic field of the brain.

The "feeling" comes from the brain's electrical and magnetic energy turned into chemicals through an emotion. The way you feel comes from your heart, and we know the heart is the most powerful source of electrical and magnetic energy. In the process of manifestation, creation starts in mind and allows the heart's powerful magnetic feeling to convert matter from the nonphysical into the physical, turning nothing into something. It's the feeling that turns the quantum field's infinite possibilities of waves and frequencies into particles of matter.

"The Marriage of your thought and emotion is the feeling, and feeling is the prayer."

- Greg Bredan

For example, if you like to manifest your favourite car, you need to tune in to this highly intelligent field as awareness and visualize driving your favourite car, visualize every detail of it, from the interior to the exterior of how you like it and combine this thought with an elevated emotion of love, gratitude and contentment and feel as if that car has already manifested into your reality and you own it and feel grateful for it, and the feeling is the language that you use to command the universe or the quantum field to deliver what you have asked for.

When we understand the language, this field communicates with us is the "feeling," what if we all prayed to God from this present perspective? As if it has already happened. When we seek help from God, we ask from a place of absence and victimhood, thus getting in return more of absence. If I have to pray to God for my healing, I will have to pray from a perspective and feeling that he has already blessed me with healing.

When we go from being human to being "superhuman," we gain access to the power within us to create and manifest life on purpose and our own will. We do this by consciously creating thought and the right kind of feeling in this invisible web of waves and frequencies. Abiding by laws of quantum physics when you create this loop of thought-emotion-feeling and become aware of this, you give life to your desire and as much as you linger in this loop with gratitude, this will break into particles of matter and magnetize the desired future toward you.

Entering Into the Quantum Field

The normal state of consciousness we use to access this physical reality is constrictive, like pinpointed focus. Our focus on the physical reality sharpens down to only one point at a time, blurring everything around. This state of consciousness is great for survival purposes, as it keeps us alert about our surroundings by constantly keeping our eyes open for any threat. With this type of consciousness, you can well manoeuvre around the physical world. But to tap into this highly intelligent quantum field, you cannot enter with a constrictive focus. You need to build an expansive focus to enter into the quantum field so that you can rest your attention on waves and frequencies. The best way to do this is by practising resting your focus on the empty space around your body. By doing this, you not only tap into the quantum field but also lower your brain waves to access your intuition.

One good exercise you can do whenever you find a sweet alone spot during the day is close your eyes and practice resting your focus and awareness on the empty space around you. You will feel a sense of peace and relaxation at the moment and also learn to tune in to the quantum field more easily and effectively.

The Changes in The Brain and Body When You Invest Your Awareness into The Present Moment or The Quantum Field.

Once we slip into the quantum field and become aware of this infinite field of information where there is nothing physical but only waves and frequencies, we understand that we move our narrow focus from objects, people, places, things, or time in our outer world to an expansive focus into the vastness of this infinite emptiness by putting our attention on nothing, on empty space, energy and information, and that's when our brain starts to change.

Now, the brain's separate parts are starting to come together and move towards coherence and harmony. When the brain becomes coherent, so does the body.

When we enter the quantum field of waves and energy, the second thing that happens to our brain is that our brain waves slow down, from beta to alpha to theta (we will understand brainwaves in detail on the next page). This is important because when we slow down our brain waves, our consciousness moves out of the thinking neocortex and into the midbrain (the limbic brain), where it connects with the "autonomic nervous system or ANS."

The Autonomic Nervous System

The ANS is the body's subconscious operating system. This part of the nervous system is in charge of digesting food, making hormones, regulating body temperature, controlling blood sugar, keeping the heart beating, making antibodies that fight infections, repairing damaged cells, and doing many other things that most mainstream scientists think we don't have conscious control over. The ANS is really what keeps you alive. Its main job is to keep the brain and body in balance by bringing order and homeostasis to them.

The more we stay in the present moment or the quantum field, the different parts of our brains work together and create balance. When this happens, the ANS starts to heal the body. It breaks down food more effectively, controls the heartbeat and blood pressure, instructs glands to make the chemicals needed to heal the body, and does much more. When the body is stressed and produces cortisol and adrenaline, the ANS shuts down, causing problems like poor digestion, irregular heartbeats, high blood pressure, diabetes and even cancer. To keep the ANS actively participating in the healing process of the body, all we have to do is stay tuned into the present moment or the quantum field as much as we can.

Brain Waves and Their Key to Embracing The Superhuman

Knowing how to alter your brain waves is essential if you need to mentally isolate yourself from the rest of the world to access the quantum field. Talking about the frequency of brain waves they are divided into five distinct categories

Beta (16-24Hz), Alpha (8-16Hz), Theta (4-8Hz), Delta (0-4Hz) and Gamma (24-100Hz)

There are low, medium, and high beta ranges that can be measured. If you're in low-range beta, you're at ease, not worried about anything happening in the outside world but nevertheless aware of your body in physical reality. When you pay attention in a casual chat, or focus on a teacher's lecture, your brain waves will be in the lower beta range.

Think of stress in the mid-beta range as positive, as when you're a little worried about a loved one and talking to them about their sickness. When stress chemicals like cortisol and adrenaline flood the body, it enters a condition of high-range beta brain waves. These types of brain activity are seen in people experiencing intense emotional states, including pain, sadness, worry, frustration, or despair.

Even if you spend most of your working day at beta brain wave frequency, you will also experience brief periods of alpha brain wave frequency. Alpha waves are produced in the brain when a person feels at ease, creative, or intuitive. If beta brain waves show that you are focusing on the external world most of the time, alpha brain waves suggest you are focusing on your inner world while daydreaming or visualizing something wonderful. This brain frequency is also experienced when you are performing creative tasks like painting, listening to music or writing.

When your body is starting to drift off to sleep, entering into a dreamy trance state, you are in the theta range of brain waves. Intense meditative experiences are linked to this frequency. It's been said that this is the doorway to your subconscious mind. It's when your brain goes into a profound trance. This is the brain wave induced by hypno or psycho-therapists to tap into and heal your subconscious mind.

It is common for our brain waves to dip into the delta range while we are deep asleep. However, specialists in meditation have been shown to enter a deep delta state of mind when meditating too.

I would characterize the gamma brain wave frequency as indicative of a superconscious state. When the brain becomes alert due to some internal stimulus, it releases energy at high frequencies. It is also often documented soon after a traumatic event, such as a car accident, or after a very intense spiritual experience by a meditator. One develops a sense that time is slowing down. A lot of powerful breathing techniques and chants are used to access these deep levels of brain waves.

As we learnt earlier, one of the most powerful techniques to consciously lower your brain waves is by laying your focus on the emptiness around you. This simple technique lowers your brain waves into alpha and theta and makes it easy for you to access the quantum field as an awareness. When you master this one technique, you are halfway there, becoming superhuman. We will use this technique by the end of the book to help you create your personalized meditation.

The Power of Emotion and Belief

A few years back, I had a client come to me seeking help for her relationship and career. She was an attractive 28year-old woman. She said in a span of ten years, she had six devastatingly heartbroken relationships, saying all the men she met have consistently cheated on her, and now as she got married, she is barely in a place to trust her husband. She reached a universally famous understanding that many women have, "all men are dogs," which reminded me of my dog and its loyalty with a smile, and I listened further to what she had to say. She also mentioned how difficult her life is when it comes to finances. No matter how hard she tried, she could barely have any money in her hand left and barely managed to meet ends. She mentioned how messed up of a relationship she has with her mother, and both barely even talk to each other for years. Overall, I realized this young woman is a bundle of negative emotions and beliefs. I assigned her another session for intervention, and I was not surprised to outline almost all of her issues leading to her childhood. As I intervened in her childhood, I got to know that her late father was abusive and disloyal in nature. Time and again, she saw her mother suffer due to her father's cheating affairs. She was also abused by her father, who often criticised her for being a burden on the family and is responsible for her family's financial conditions. As she grew up, she attracted all men who were abusive and disloyal in nature because of this one negative emotion she had installed in her mind during her childhood. She also built a belief in her subconscious mind that she is worthless and money is difficult to acquire; due to this damaging belief, she could barely succeed in her professional life. Regarding her relationship with her mother (which was good until a few years back), when I intervened, I outlined an event where she mentioned she desperately wanted to get into acting a few years back, and when she got a role, her mother refused her to pursue her dream. This was enough to see the negative emotion she built regarding her mother.

Outlining all these issues in her subconscious mind, I ran her through a therapy called the NLP Negative Emotion Timeline therapy for her mother and father and an NLP Belief change therapy for her career and finances (I will take you in-depth of NLP psychotherapies in the next chapter). When I helped her release these years and decades-old negative emotions and damaging beliefs, she reported after a few weeks how magically normal her relationship with her mom became and how her relationship with her husband has become, how she trusts her man now and the thought of disloyalty flew away from the marriage. She also happened to get through a job interview in an esteemed organization that she has desired to work for a long time. She said she now feels more empowered and had never felt this light and relieved in years and, how less foggy her mind became, how she had more energy in her body. There are countless such people whom I have coached and consulted in the past few years who were beautiful souls but were entangled in endless cycles of emotional and mental misery due to just one or two negative emotions and a few damaging beliefs.

The power of emotions and beliefs in our bodies and life is undefinable. One negative emotion is enough to take your life off course, and one damaging belief can hold you down for your entire life. (You will learn in more depth about belief in "the placebo" next chapter).

How Emotions and Beliefs are Auto Manifestation Programs

As we learnt earlier, the amount of electromagnetic field your brain and heart generate on average in a period of twenty-four hours is said to be your electromagnetic signature field or your average energy field. Once these negative emotions get hardwired in your subconscious mind, they become the body, and these emotions are just waiting for any external event or random negative thought to trigger them. Your body goes into an emotional turmoil and, in turn, makes your heart vibrate an electromagnetic field that is low in cycles and manifest everything low vibrational in life, from disloyal partners to difficult and low-paying jobs to illnesses in the body. Once these emotions are in constant motion, they get periodically timed in your body clock as well, and you may wonder why so many times you are simply relaxing and your body automatically starts feeling low and depressed, and you know the chemicals in your gut are at work. In this case, you might have felt exactly the same yesterday at the same time or the same time last week or the same time last month. These sixty to hundred thoughts per minute running in your mind out of awareness now become products of these emotions. The same case is with beliefs. A belief is technically a feeling that is hardwired because of an event in your life that you felt and perceived to be very true; it could also be a perception of someone else that you accepted to be true. For example, the 28-year-old woman who was constantly blamed for being the reason for her family's financial misery throughout her childhood to her adolescence accepted and believed money is difficult and she is not worth having in abundance. This belief vibrating deep in her subconscious mind was enough to keep her life in financial misery or relationship disloyalty in cycles no matter how hard she tried. That is why doing an emotional check and belief check periodically is very important to keep your electromagnetic signature field always high.

Negative emotions, phobias, damaging beliefs, and psychosomatic illnesses are stored as patterns in your subconscious mind.

Any emotion that makes you unhappy and wretched is referred to as a negative emotion. These feelings cause you to despise both yourself and other people, which lowers your level of self-assurance, self-worth, and overall life pleasure.

Hatred, wrath, jealousy, and grief are some unpleasant emotions that might develop. However, these emotions are quite normal in the appropriate situation. Depending on how long we allow negative emotions to impact us and how we choose to express them, they may reduce our overall zest for life.

The impact of negative emotions on our bodies and life can be one of the biggest tyrannies of one's life. Majorly, as we understood earlier, these negative emotions have their roots in one's childhood. For example, a child that has been abandoned or a child that has not been loved enough is bound to have damaged relationships in his or her adulthood. Also, a child that has always been mocked down by his close ones and constantly been defined by unworthiness has all the possibility to have a struggling life and career.

These experiences get stored in one's mind in the form of complex neurological patterns and impact one's life till their grave or till one consciously chooses to heal. With the help of psychotherapies, these negative emotions can be uninstalled in a matter of five to ten minutes, and you stand a chance to experience and craft a life beyond these negative emotional states.

Negative feelings kept inside lead to a downward spiral.

When we are feeling bad, we can't think, act, or see things as they really are, especially when a hard-wired negative emotion or feeling has taken over the mind and body.

In such situations, we frequently see and recall just the things we want to notice. We are unable to appreciate life. As a result, just prolongs our anger or sadness. The issue only becomes worse as time passes in this situation. Inappropriately managing unpleasant emotions, such as expressing anger violently, can also be damaging. Expressing any emotion from the language of the subconscious mind refers to learning the valuable lessons behind the main event. Lessons can be powerful and are capable of helping you transcend a specific negative emotion. For example, if you have lost a loved one, it is important for you to learn the lessons behind the loss. The lessons could be how blessed you were to have his or her presence in your life, how the one you lost has made your life better etc. Learning "positive" lessons from every experience should be the epitome of every experience to live an emotionally healthy life.

Our bodies' biochemical and physiological systems engage in a variety of complicated reactions known as "emotions." Hormones and chemicals are released by our brain and body in response to our thoughts, arousing us. Positive or negative emotions all arise in this manner. It's a difficult process as the language of the subconscious mind is repetition; either you become conscious enough to contraindicate your negative emotion with a positive lesson a minimum of twenty-one times being conscious, or the other easy way is therapy.

This happened a year and a half back when I had lost one of the most valued treasures I had, my father. It was 3:00 a.m. when a doctor from the intensive critical care unit called me into the waiting room and asked me to take a seat with a heavy voice, and the energy around him was evident for me to know what he was about to say. He mentions in a very sad tone that my father has failed to revive the surgery shock and is now only on machine support. He had lost all his vitals, and it was time to let him go gracefully. I heard every word he said and asked him if I could see my father one last time before they unplugged him from the life support system. I told the doctor I just wanted to stand in front of him, close my eyes and say a little prayer. As the doctor agreed, I walked into the intensive care unit and looked at my father and closed my eyes. In my inner world of sadness that was building at a rapid pace, I stood conscious, knowing the nature of the subconscious mind. I knew if I did not meet this experience of my life from the emotion of love, I would suffer endlessly, losing this treasure. My conscious self reminded me of my power to transcend any sadness and use what I preached best. I took a deep and relaxing breath, and, in my mind, I floated out of my body six feet above and took a drone view of my father and me, looking at this event from four different perspectives (NLP technique). Saw him and cherished him for the last time in this physical world and told myself how fortunate I was to have my father next to me in his last few months, how fortunate I was to have a father who loved me to the moon and back till the age of thirty-six, I reminded myself of my friends and cousins who had lost their fathers in their childhood and how blessed I was. My mind started flashing all the beautiful memories I had with my father, and I honoured him; I honoured the way he lived his life, the pillars of integrity he stood on, and the effort he put behind giving me the best life and I took a deep breath with a tear rolling down my eye, I opened my eyes and asked the doctor, shall I inform my family about the demise? He sadly said yes. I walked out of the intensive care unit feeling thankful for this man's presence in my life, feeling thankful for being a part of me and feeling thankful for every bit of love he poured on me. As the famous Canadian psychologist Jordan Peterson says, "You have to be the strongest person at your father's funeral." it made me understand what strength truly is!

As the grief dissolved with time, I still was conscious enough to choose love over sadness, cherishing every memory and not letting his absence change the love he had for me or the love I have for him. In fact, as I reached home, I told my wife, "My father became closer to me today," and she knew what I meant.

This is the power of being conscious and not letting events in your life destroy you emotionally. I encourage you or anyone who has gone through an event losing their loved one and is incapable of battling the loss please refer to a psychotherapist to uninstall the negative emotion you built during the event and set yourself free from the damaging emotion and cherish your loved one with pure love and no sadness. If these sorts of emotions linger in your mind and body, your brain and heart will be in a loop of creating and manifesting more and more loss in every aspect of your life.

How to handle unpleasant thoughts, emotions and feelings on the go.

The backbone of transcendental meditation is the **fourfold breath**. The easiest pocket tool to curb anxiety and unpleasant emotions at the moment. This specific breathing pattern originates from the science that explains an intrinsic connection between breath and thought. Have you noticed how your breathing becomes relaxed and deep when you are thinking about something pleasant and beautiful? or have you noticed how your breathing will change to short and stressed when you think of something dangerous or horrific? Try this right now as you are reading this book, close your eyes for two minutes, think of something beautiful that has recently happened to you and notice how your breathing changes to calm and slow.

Then think about something unpleasant that happened to you recently; you will see how your breath changes its tune accordingly.

The science behind this powerful pocket tool is this, when you feel extremely stressed out or depressed, **close your eyes and relax your body from head to toe while taking a deep and comfortable breath on a count of four and holding your breath on a count of four, then exhale on the count of four and hold for a count of four and repeat this process for a few times**. You will see how your depressive and anxious thoughts dissolve effortlessly, tuning in with your conscious breathing pattern. You can use this tool as many times as you need in the day, and you will notice in a short period of time you probably would not even need this pocket tool.

There are also several other coping mechanisms available to deal with unpleasant feelings. These consist of the following:

- Exercise: aerobic activity reduces stress hormone levels and improves your ability to handle unpleasant emotions.

- Don't overthink situations by going over them again in your thoughts. Rather, close your eyes and visualize the best possible result of the event that is making you anxious.

- In order to be ready in advance, learn to recognize how sadness, loss, and rage make you feel and which circumstances cause them and learn the lessons behind these emotions.

- Don't dwell on the horrible things that happened in the past; doing so steals your present and makes you feel bad. Practice detachment. Know that it happened in the past and it holds no place in your present.

- Try to be rational, acknowledge that unpleasant emotions might happen from time to time, and consider measures to improve your mood or seek therapy.

- Use relaxing activities to unwind, such as meditating, reading, listening to soothing instrumental music or conversing with a friend.

Phobias

An excessive and unreasonable fear response is known as a phobia. If you have a phobia, you might feel extreme dread or panic when you come in contact with the thing that makes you afraid. An object, circumstance, or location might be the source of the fear. A phobia often has a specific connection as opposed to more general anxiety problems.

A phobia may have effects that are somewhat bothersome or extremely crippling. Many times, phobia sufferers are aware that their dread is unreasonable, yet they are helpless to change it. Hormonal health, work, study, and interpersonal interactions may all be hampered by such worries.

Causes

Phobias can be brought on by environmental and genetic causes. Children are more likely to acquire phobias if they have a close family member who suffers from an anxiety illness. Fear can develop as a result of distressing experiences, like almost drowning. Phobias can be brought on by exposure to small places, great heights, and animal or insect stings. Phobias are also frequently present in individuals with continuous medical illnesses or health issues. Following traumatic brain injuries, phobias are very common in humans. Phobias are also linked to despair and substance misuse.

The symptoms of phobias are distinct from those of severe mental diseases like schizophrenia. People with schizophrenia have unpleasant symptoms, disorganized symptoms, delusions, paranoia, and visual and auditory hallucinations. Although phobias may be illogical, those who have them do not do poorly on tests of reality.

A fear that interferes with their daily lives affects an estimated nineteen million Americans. If you have a phobia that keeps you from living life to the fullest, you can visit our website and do the phobia cure therapy meditation by simply plugging on your earphones and experiencing the impact in your life.

Damaging Belief

Different beliefs can affect our minds and body in different ways. Some beliefs could be considered "constructive" because they improve our ability to adapt to our surroundings, give us a sense of self-worth, and generally lead to greater physical and mental health. Some ideas are deemed "destructive" because they make us more stressed, harm our health, or inspire hostility and aggressive sentiments in others. One of the key factors in determining whether beliefs are constructive or harmful is whether they exclude or reject alternative points of view and how strongly they are held. We also understood earlier in this book belief is one of the most powerful energy impulses or feeling that the heart can produce, and if the feeling is the prayer, what are we creating for ourselves if we linger more in the destructive frame of belief?

Looking at both sides of belief, which are constructive and destructive, both play a huge role in impacting our own lives. The most dreaded belief that I have seen in my clients that hinders their healing in every way is the belief that the human life span is 60–80 years. As recent science reveals, "mind is over matter" We need to understand the power of our mind when subjected to a belief. When one has a belief that has been drilled into his or her mind since childhood that when you cross sixty, you're heading towards your grave, the enslaved body in command of this master mind will strap itself with a time bomb to explode anywhere between 60–80. If you are someone who is suffering to heal from an illness or disease and finding it difficult to heal it, you might as well look into your belief about the average human life span. I do not deny the statistical report that says the average human life span is 60–80 years, but all I am trying to say is, why don't you believe you are one of those lucky ones who crossed a hundred joyfully and healthy?

Another example of a destructive belief that I have witnessed in countless people is the belief that the opposite gender is a crook. Sounds funny, but yes, we all have heard this, every man is a dog, or every woman is a cheat etc.; if your mind has a destructive belief like this, how would you manifest a relationship that is actually meant for you? As we learnt earlier, this belief will not only manifest all the wrong dogs and cheaters in your life but put you into deep states of distress and depression and eventually crumple all the other areas of your life. As long as a belief vibrates in your brain as a neurological pattern, you keep attracting the same people and experiences in your life in cycles of misery because the law of attraction and magnetism is irrespectively working for you.

If you think you have a belief that is hindering any aspect of your life, be it your career growth, be it your intimate relationships or your overall health, be assured that you are just one therapy away from manifesting the life that you desire.

What exactly is a psychosomatic illness?

A psychosomatic disorder is a psychological ailment that causes physical symptoms to appear but typically has no known medical cause. People with this illness may worry, feel, or think too much about their symptoms, which can make it hard for them to do even the most normal things in life.

Typically, people with psychosomatic disorders don't disclose overt signs of mental discomfort. Instead, they think that their issues are brought on by underlying medical ailments. They routinely seek testing and treatments from healthcare professionals but frequently go without a diagnosis, which can be upsetting and distressing to most. Somatic symptom disorder, somatic symptoms, and somatic pain are other names for psychosomatic disorders.

In simple words, these types of illnesses have their roots in the mind and not in the body and healing these ailments using pharmaceutical medication is nothing but a temporary solution. To heal this from the root again, you are just a therapy away.

How common is a condition with somatic symptoms?

A prevalent illness known as somatic symptom disorder affects 5%–7% of the general population. Though a lot of other illnesses may have first originated in the body, it is very likely to be turned psychosomatic in a brief amount of time enduring it. So, it is important to note that, even after healing from a specific physical ailment, your mind needs healing, too, in order to not manifest the same illness all over again.

Studies show that the following things may make a person more likely to have somatic symptoms:

- Erratic way of life.

- A problem with understanding and expressing emotions.

- Previous sexual abuse.

- Other mental problems, such as depression or personality disorders.

- Abusing drugs (such as alcoholism or drug addiction).

- Major medical surgeries

For many known reasons, women experience somatic discomfort around ten times more frequently than males.

What Happens After a Trauma?

In 2019, a dear friend called me in a state of emergency, saying his brother had been through an emotional breakdown due to the fake allegations he was arrested for. He suffered months of harassment from the court, from the cops, from the local goons and had reached a point his mental health had deteriorated to a great extent. As I intervened in his situation, it was clear to see the poor man was suffering from post-traumatic stress disorder. As they had consulted a psychiatrist, he got hooked on sedatives and stayed calm only when he was on a higher dose day after day. His life began to crumple in ways nobody imagined. He describes how even a phone or the doorbell ringing could put him into fight or flight and how anybody speaking to him in a slightly raised voice could get his body into deep states of stress, anxiety and fear, although the incident of his arrest and harassment happened months ago and it was all legally settled in court. He said, "It is now impossible for me to drive during bright daylight as the moment I get on a steering wheel, I feel I am going to be attacked or followed or arrested, and I often start to tremble and panic." He also mentioned irrespective of his mind knowing that all of this was over, he still couldn't stay away from the emotional breakdowns he was constantly facing.

When the brain suffers from intense amounts of stress and anxiety in an event, be it short or long, it forms deep wired neurological patterns and networks related to that event and, more than often, harms the physical body. It gets on a mode of finding any external trigger to activate the whole emotional roll all over again. Sometimes, these emotional roles can cost days to calm down. Our prefrontal cortex is the logical hub of the brain, where all of these cognitive processes (including the interpretation of language) take place. The prefrontal cortex may shut down when individuals enter a "fight, flight, or freeze" response after experiencing trauma. Because of the overwhelming nature of trauma, the brain becomes disordered, and the higher thinking and language processes of the brain shut down so that the body can focus on survival. The metabolic shutdown causes a severe, permanently stored stress reaction.

Post-traumatic stress disorder (PTSD) affects one quarter of every 100 people who have experienced trauma. Given these numbers, we know this is not a disease but rather a typical reaction to a very stressful circumstance and healing it from the roots is healing the subconscious mind. It took me a few therapies and a personalized meditation to undo his mental turmoil.

Law of Cause and Effect in Regards to Pain & Healing

You might have already heard a lot about this famous law in the self-help communities. Here is how it reached my understanding,

One day when I was hammering a nail on my wall at home to hang a painting, I accidentally hammered my finger, and the pain was to hell and back at that moment.

Then it felt better after a few minutes. I realized I was not angry and handled the pain as if it was my own making my own mistake. The healing was not too painful and long, as my mind knew it was caused by me. This is because my mind accepted being at CAUSE and not at EFFECT.

Similarly, another day I was working with my colleague trying to fix something that broke at the office as a helpful gesture, and while he was trying to hammer and fix something I was holding tight, he accidentally hammered my finger, and at that moment the pain felt like a ride to hell, and back again, I burst out in anger screaming at him for being careless and reckless for hurting me. The pain seemed horrible for hours and took much longer to heal, and the journey to this healing was a painful experience as my mind knew I was the victim here because the pain was caused by another.

It was that I was living on the "effect" side of the "law of cause & effect."

I was feeling victimized for being hurt by another's carelessness. I had often cursed my colleague for days till I was completely healed.

Similarly, imagine if you are a smoker, and you know those burns and accidental stubs we do to our hands and legs; how does it feel? And if someone else stubs their cigarette on you. How different is the pain in both these situations?

Or imagine how different is the emotional pain when you abuse yourself in a mirror and when someone else abuses you on your face? When technically, in both situations, you were abused.

Being at CAUSE keeps you on higher energy than being at EFFECT.

Being at CAUSE gives you peace,

Being at EFFECT gives you only stress and pain.

Being at CAUSE, your body heals out of any physical pain or emotional pain faster than being at EFFECT because of the chemicals released in the body in both experiences. We will learn in chapters ahead how the chemicals produced in the human body can either heal a person or even kill a person.

Modern science, as we learned, explains the mind and matter connection and clearly states how our mind creates the entirety of our physical reality. This means being at CAUSE will help you stay away from that pain in your future, whereas staying at EFFECT will only attract and create more of such painful experiences and nothing else.

In life, we get hurt by so many other people, and we constantly live in states of anger, regret & heavy stress, but the truth is every experience in our physical reality is a construct of our own mind. So, taking a conscious responsibility in realizing the experience that sprung out of your mind and the other who hurt you is just a manifestation of your thoughts and emotions will help you switch to CAUSE from being at EFFECT.

The societal conditioning and programming we go through from being a child to an adult are to be at EFFECT, and every time we get hurt physically or emotionally, we operate from being at EFFECT.

The world teaches us that we are victims of this creation, but in reality, we are victims of our own creation.

The day we experience being creators of our reality is when we cross the lines from being human to being superhuman. Being at CAUSE is being conscious. Being at EFFECT is a subconscious mind activity, which is nothing but an auto-run program.

The Buddhists preached about the wheel of Samsara; the cycles of endless creation refer to being at EFFECT in a repetitive cycle over and over again till you become conscious of your mind and realize that you are the creator of your own individual reality and you consciously choose to break out of the cycle of the victimized effect.

————◆————

Chapter - 4

Neurolinguistic Programming (Nlp)

What Is NLP, exactly?

The field of neuro-linguistic programming largely investigates how our thoughts, beliefs and emotions influence our overall life. It examines how our brains perceive messages and how these interpretations influence our actions. The linguistic component of neuro-linguistic programming is how it does this. NLP approaches to assist us in viewing our thoughts, feelings, and emotions as things we can influence rather than things that passively happen to us by looking at how our brains process information.

One of my strongest views and understanding about NLP is it is a subject everyone has to learn and practice in order to live the life they deserve. Summing up the significance of this one subject, it is enough to heal most of your emotional miseries and beliefs that have influence over your life in almost every way using the power of Psychotherapies.

What Does Neurolinguistic Programming Do?

NLP approaches are utilized for a wide range of objectives since they centre on changing behaviour. To treat depression and anxiety, mental health practitioners utilize NLP alone or in combination with other forms of treatment, such as talk therapy or psychoanalysis. As we understood earlier, negative emotions, damaging beliefs, decades-old phobias, traumas, unresourceful likes and dislikes, painful behaviours, damaging habits, psychosomatic illnesses, relationship issues and much more are merely a ten-minute therapy away from being completely healed from your life if you consult the right therapist.

A new map will be created by the therapist to replace the old one with empowered routines and practical tactics. The therapist will try to find the person's "map," which is made up of unhelpful patterns in the subconscious mind that make us feel stuck and using the science of NLP linguistics, uninstall those patterns and, if needed, install beneficial and resourceful patterns in our subconscious mind.

Those who are interested in personal growth—a strong human desire that can bring meaning to our lives— but do not have a major mental health problem will definitely benefit from neurolinguistic programming as well. Skills like public speaking, sales and negotiation, team building, and leadership may all be improved with NLP communication approaches.

NLP and coaching go hand in hand because of their action-oriented nature and emphasis on progress. Several coaches use NLP techniques to help their clients change the way their minds work and reach their goals.

NLP's Top 5 Techniques for Healing Psychological Issues

NLP focuses on "how to respond" rather than the "why to respond", like you might in therapy. Instead of asking why, consider how you might respond differently to your thoughts and feelings. How can you modify your communication approach to fit the circumstances? How can you alter your perspective so that life occurs "for you" rather than "to you"?

Imagery Skills

One of the most well-known visualization-based neurolinguistic programming approaches is imagery training, often known as a mental rehearsal. Because it is simple and linear, it's a great workout for beginners. The secret is to imagine oneself completing an activity effectively being fully associated (visualizing seeing from your own eyes), whether it is giving a presentation at work or going for a date or a meeting with your boss, visualizing the successful end and feeling it as if it has happened, will more than often bring a positive result in your life's important events. It is also one very good way to dissolve any anxiety building up for the shortcoming event.

For example, if I have to give a seminar on a stage in Infront of a large audience tomorrow, I will sit with my eyes close and relax my body today and "directly visualize the end of my seminar, where I am signing off, and I see and hear my audience clap for me, and having to shake hands backstage with people thanking me for the wonderful seminar and hear them say how it has left an everlasting impact on their lives, and I feel the gratitude and compassion in my heart for these beautiful people clapping for me and appreciating my presence," and I open my eyes. This process might not take any more than five to eight minutes of your time, but it is very powerful and effective in order to let loose some anxiety and, as we learnt, manifesting the best possible outcome.

From a quantum science perspective, as we learned earlier in this book, you are pre-programming or priming your brain for already having a neural circuitry ready for your desired successful outcome, and you create a feeling in the quantum field of already achieving what you desire.

NLP Swish

This one technique can help you change your behaviour pattern on the go. For example, if something is making you feel bad over and over again and you want to break this cycle, take a deep breath, relax your body and close your eyes. Ask yourself,

When you feel bad about this event, do you have a picture?

A picture will pop up on your mind screen; memorize that picture in your mind.

Now ask yourself again, how would you like to feel instead? A picture will pop up on your mind screen again,

If you see yourself in the desired state's picture, perfect, don't make any changes. If you don't see yourself in the picture, set the picture as you can see yourself in the image (Disassociated view-looking at yourself from your own eyes).

Increase the contrast and the brightness of the picture in your mind and memorize this second picture.

Clear your mind screen while you keep your eyes closed

Take picture one and visualize it big on your mind screen; if you don't see yourself, perfect; if not, step into the picture being fully associated (fully associated-looking from your own eyes) and adjust the second picture to small, tiny and bright on the down-left corner. (Make sure you are dis-associated and you can see yourself in the picture)

Have the second picture (small on the corner) expand big in a second and break and completely cover the old picture, and say "swish" as you do it. Now clear your mind screen and repeat this process of breaking picture one and covering it with picture two, four to five times minimum, or until you sense the feeling is no longer accessible.

By using this technique in the right way, you can easily change your behaviour and feeling regarding any event that troubles you.

Modelling

Successful businesspeople, sportsmen, and others have paid the most attention to modelling as an NLP training strategy. It is predicated on the law of attraction, which says you manifest what you repeatedly think about and focus on. You must surround yourself with individuals who have attained the success you desire and concentrate on adopting their behaviours if you want to improve your life. You can seek out a mentor, join a mastermind group, or follow in the footsteps of a CEO or executive you look up to.

Mirroring

The 7-38-55 Rule states that just 7% of your message should be expressed verbally. While your vocal tone accounts for 38% of your message, your body language accounts for 55%. Mirroring is an NLP approach that uses body language to establish rapport and relationships with anyone. Try to mimic the other person's body language when speaking to them. Match their level of energy if they have a lot of it. Reflect on their calm body language if you notice it. Even your word choice may be modified to fit their language. Because you are similar to the other person, they will instantly trust you more and drop their wall of ego and judgement.

These are just a few things out of the world of NLP tools that could be done during a coaching or neurolinguistic programming session.

How to Use NLP for Self-Help Step 1 NLP

Create uplifting objectives. Focus on what you want rather than what you don't want as you begin making plans for your future. Don't set negative objectives for items you wish to get or avoid. Instead, consider your desired goals, aspirations, and personal growth. Craft your objectives such that they accurately reflect all of your desires. For instance, if you desire a spouse, change your aim to "Live my life with someone I genuinely love" from "Stay away from the wrong ones" Or if you have to want a new car, don't say I don't want to drive this old car, rather say I would love to drive that new car as it is already mine!

Instead of just saying that you will take a step in the plan, you will be more likely to reach a goal if you think it will be fun.

Step 2 NLP

Ask yourself encouraging questions. NLP uses self squestioning as a core technique. Ask questions about the aspects of your life that you would like to alter. Your mind will attempt to provide answers to any questions you ask, so be careful to formulate your inquiries in a manner that will result in insightful, uplifting responses. For instance, you can ask, "What can I do to feel better?" rather than "What's wrong with me?"

As Dr Joseph Murphy says in the book, "Power of your subconscious mind," the self-questioning technique is the best to be performed in a hypnotic state, for example, just before you sleep or right when you wake up or during your meditation practice.

Step 3 NLP

Edit the pictures in your head. NLP experts contend that seeing people, situations, or other things may help you comprehend how you feel about them. Imagine a person or something that bothers you in order to accomplish this. Next, alter the mental picture as if you were using a computer to modify it. Imagine the things or people that make you unhappy becoming darker and disappearing. Imagine the people or things that bring you joy, brightening and advancing toward you.

Considering your feelings in light of all these developments is very important.

Step 4 of NLP

Play with the negative thoughts in your brain. Your happiness and mental health have a lot to do with how you talk to yourself in your thoughts. The majority of psychologists would advise you to become aware of how you are speaking to yourself and to switch to a loving and supportive voice. NLP takes a different track, suggesting you alter the negative voice's tone to lessen its influence.

If you catch yourself saying to yourself, "You'll never finish this," repeat the sentence with a distorted voice. Make it seem silly, like Donald Duck or SpongeBob from a cartoon. Take note of how various voices make you feel.

Step 5 of NLP

Replay situations in reverse. Treat a negative event that is bothering you like a movie. Play it backwards, beginning from the end moment to its start in dull colour contrast or black and white. Repeat this multiple times until you can memorize and recall the reversed order.

Take note of your feelings about the encounter.

Step 6 of NLP

If you have a negative thought that looks uncomfortable or threatening in nature and you feel it may manifest unnecessarily by vibrating it more, say to yourself in your mind or verbally, "Program reject," and visualize squeezing the thought into a tiny black ball and pushing that ball towards your back with your hand while creating a mechanical crank shift noise in your head and toss it far over the horizon of your past and create a sound of something crashing or breaking as it crosses the horizon. You will see how your mind and body stop reacting to the uneasiness of that unfamiliar thought. If you feel the negative thought to be very dominant, repeat this process a few times.

Epigenetics

"A cell's life is controlled by the physical and energetic environment and not by its genes. Genes are simply molecular blueprints used in the construction of cells, tissues and organs. The environment serves as a contractor" who reads and engages those blueprints and is ultimately responsible for the character of the cell's life. It is a single cells awareness of the environment, not its genes, that set into motion the mechanics of life."

~ Dr Bruce Lipton,

A Definition of Epigenetics

Epigenetics means above (epi) your genetics or gene structure. The term "gene expression" is used to describe the rate and timing of protein production in response to genetic instructions. Epigenetic modifications regulate gene expression by switching genes "on" and "off," while genetic changes determine which proteins are produced.

To understand epigenetics, let's look into what Genetics as a branch of science explains. Earlier to epigenetics as a subject to evolve, genetics held strong grounds in the medical communities expressing with utter confidence that we are slaves to the genetic disposition of our parental genes. This means if both my father and mother (or either one) had diabetes and had tremendously suffered and died because of diabetes, the genes I imbibed at birth from them will express the same diseases in me as they occurred in my parent's bodies, and I am very likely to die the same way, which held true to a great extent but failed to explain many other occasions involving parental genes. The science of epigenetics evolved not only from the arena of cellular biology or genetics but also from the new-age science of mind and matter; it proves clearly that we are not slaves to our parental genes (which were inherently passed down to us). We are slaves to our environment, an environment that signals our genes to activate or deactivate and express accordingly.

Let's look at this science from a layman's perspective; John and Linda were born to parents who suffered from obesity and diabetes. John was sent to a boarding school abroad for his education at a very young age, whereas Linda seemed fortunate to spend her childhood with her parents. As Linda reached her adolescence, she started suffering from obesity and, sooner than expected, was diagnosed with diabetes. John, on the other hand, who only visited home for fifteen days annually from his boarding school, grew up to be a physically fit and healthy man, holding barely any scope of developing obesity or diabetes. What we understand from this example is this the environment Linda was brought up in expressed obesity and diabetes, the suffering, the consequences, the pain, the diet, and the discomfort. Whereas John, on the other hand, grew up in an environment barely holding any cues related to the dormant parental genes in his cellular structure. Since John was in an environment that signalled genes to express health and vitality, the healthy genes that activated his body away from home eventually manifested a healthy life.

So, the question arises, if the environment has a direct effect on our bodies, then it takes us down the same road of enslavement; earlier, it was to the parental genes, but now it's the goddamn environment we are slaves to! Let's look at another example to feel a little bit sadder before we feel happy again. John and Linda were born to parents who were health-conscious and fitness enthusiasts. Due to some reason, Linda was adopted by John's uncle and aunt, who lived in a different city. John's uncle and aunt, both cardiac patients, suffered from their illness for years. Eventually, one of them died because of a heart attack. Linda, in her thirties, developed cardiovascular issues, and John was living a healthy and fit life. What we understand is that, for a disease to surface, one does not even need parental genes to express illness, but the environment is enough to down-regulate the genes already present in your DNA and make your cells express illness and disease. As unfair as it sounds, nature is not designed to work against us but to work for us, in our favour.

As Dr Bruce Lipton writes in his book, Biology of Belief, "We are not victims of our genes, but masters of our fates, able to create lives overflowing with peace, happiness and love". This statement surely is enough to understand that we are not in bondage to our environment either. As we learnt in the earlier chapters, the brain and heart are dumb in disguise (nature intended to benefit us this way). They do not have the capability to distinguish between an environment you are experiencing outside of you to be any different from the series of visuals or thoughts you play in your mind. As we learnt in the simple five-finger piano exercise, that demonstrated brain develops hard-wired neurological networks just by thought alone which also causes dormant genes to upregulate and activate a cellular function that is required for playing the piano explains, bypassing the environment by using the power of your mind.

What dominates the signature electromagnetic field of our body?

"It's not the gene-directed hormones and neurotransmitters that control our bodies and our minds; our belief controls our bodies, our minds and thus our lives . . . oh ye of little belief!" ~ Dr Bruce Lipton

The environment around us is influencing our genetic expression for sure, but it is the belief we build due to the repetitive events in our environment that amplify and auto manifests the misery or the blessing in cycles. In the first example, John, in his boarding school, formed a belief in his mind that illness and disease are not everyone's fate, whereas Linda at home believed that diabetes might happen to anyone, as she was the first-hand witness to her parent's illness and she eventually activated all the parental genes in her DNA responsible for obesity and diabetes. Same in the second example, Linda believed that cardiac issues are common and felt the pain of her uncle and aunt day in and day out, and eventually, "feeling is the prayer," she manifested cardiac issues in her life. It is rightly said belief is one of the most powerful feelings.

This is not only in the case of cells manifesting a healthy body because of a healthy environment or the other way around but also holds true in your overall life. Your environment triggers the health and vibration of your body's overall cellular structure in every way. As we understood in earlier chapters that the amount of energy each cell in our body generates in a span of twenty-four hours on average becomes our signature electromagnetic field, and this signature electromagnetic field is what is responsible for creating every bit of our life.

Let's look at another example. John and Linda were two children born in different families but studying in the same class in a reputed school. John belonged to a family that was generationally rich, successful and wealthy, and Linda belonged to a family that was struggling to make ends meet. As they grew up and passed out of college, John immediately found a job that was highly paid and in a reputed organization, whereas Linda suffered difficulties not only finding a high-paid job but finding a job itself despite being academically brighter than John. What is important to understand here is it was the belief Linda built during her childhood growing up witnessing a series of events in her environment made her confirm and believe that money is difficult to have, and if you have it, save it, hide it etc. and eventually manifested her belief in her professional life and career. John, on the other hand, grew up seeing money as a blessing, money as easy; he formulated a hard-wired neurological pattern and belief in his brain saying money is easy; it simply flows to me effortlessly and eventually manifests a life that provided him with high paid jobs, great organizations and great success.

Scientists went very far testing the power of belief, gene expression and "environment and a gene connection".

In 1981, Harvard psychologist Ellen Langer, PhD, performed a research study involving sixteen volunteers aged between seventy to eighty years. They were divided into two groups of eight each. The research team took up a monastery in Peterborough, New Hampshire, creatively turned it into a 20-year-old fashioned retreat. The interiors, the environmental cues, the furniture, the technology, almost everything in the monastery revealed a twenty-year back environment. The first group was invited for a five-day retreat at the monastery and were asked to feel, pretend and behave as if they were twenty-two years younger. They were all well assisted by music that was twenty years old, TV shows, games, newspapers, etc. At the beginning and the end of the retreat, the participants were tested on several measurements that accounted for brain, body and gene expression.

The second group was invited for the retreat the next week and were asked to just think and reminisce their 22year-old version but "not pretend" for a period of five days. The end of this research study reveals a shocking change in all sixteen volunteers. The old men displayed changes in height and weight. In fact, their walking styles changed to their younger version. The men reported growing taller as their posture automatically straightened, their joints became more flexible, and their fingers lengthened as their arthritis disappeared. They were also recorded to have an improvement in their eyesight and hearing, their memory sharpened, and their grip strength increased.

As their memory enhanced, they scored higher in mental cognition tests, with the first group that pretended and behaved as twenty-two years younger scoring higher than the second group that just reminisced about old days. Langer reported by the end of the research, the volunteers developed brain circuitry as if they were twenty-two years younger, their body's chemistry changed significantly, and as Langer said, the volunteers did not just feel younger now, they physically became younger; in fact, some volunteers from group one threw away their walking sticks while they rejoiced to play as a two-decade younger person. Dr Joe questions in his book "You Are the Placebo," "What happened in their bodies to produce such striking transformation? What could be responsible for all the measurable changes in the physical structure of these sixteen volunteers, and says, The answer is genes!" each volunteer re-activated their genes, up-regulating them, as they were twenty-two years back.

If you think mental thought, elevated feelings, behaviour and environment cause significant genetic changes in the body, an experiment conducted on healthy gene expression demonstrated the effect of physical exercise on upregulating genes responsible for health. This research study conducted in Sweden involved twenty-three participants who were slightly overweight. For a period of six months, these participants were asked to attend an aerobic session, twisting and flexing their bodies for a period of one hour twice per week. After the period of six months, researchers at Lund University noticed a whopping upregulation of 7000 genes in each participant, almost thirty per cent of genes of the entire human genome.

So the question arises when we talk about gene expression and DNA activity in all scenarios of life; science claims that we only actively use 1.5% of our entire DNA storage, and the rest 98.5% is declared as junk DNA. It makes me think about what could possibly be stored in that dormant 98.5%. Could that hold keys to higher degrees of superhuman? In my understanding, perhaps yes. Dr Joe Dispenza concludes the understanding of this new science in relation to each one of us,

"*What if nothing is changing in your external environment? What if you do the same thing with the same people at exactly the same time every day- leading to the same experiences that produce the same emotions that signal the same genes in the same way? We could say that as long as you perceive your life through the lens of your past and react to the conditions with the same neural architecture and from the same level of mind, you are headed towards a very specific, predetermined genetic destiny. In addition, what you believe about yourself, your life, and the choices you make as a result of those beliefs also keep sending the same messages to the same genes. Only when the cell is ignited in a new way by new information can it create thousands of variations of the same gene to rewrite a new expression of proteins—which changes your body. You may not be able to control all the elements in your outer world, but you can manage many aspects of your inner world. Your belief, your perceptions, and how you interact with your external environment have an influence on your internal environment, which is still the external environment of the cell. This means you—not your preprogramed biology—hold the keys to your genetic destiny. It's just a matter of finding the right key that fits into the right lock to unleash your potential. So why not see your genes for what they really are? Providers of possibility, resources of unlimited potential, a code system of personal commands—in truth, they are nothing short of tools for transformation, which literally means changing form."*

~ You are the Placebo

Gratitude, and The Elevated Emotions Experiment

The famous story of a gratitude stone in the book "the secret" by Rhonda Byrne talks about an experience when Lee Brower, a transformational coach and author, was suffering from a ton of professional and personal issues in his life, and one day he understood the power of gratitude and decided to dedicate a small smooth little stone he found on the sidewalk to be his gratitude stone and kept it in his pocket everywhere he went out. He promised himself that whenever he touched this stone in his pocket, he would express gratitude for something he was already blessed with. As he did this for a brief amount of time, his life magically changed, and he got healthier and more successful. One day, he met an African man and accidentally dropped his gratitude stone in front of him and out of curiosity, the African man enquires humbly why a stone in Lee's pocket. Lee describes the stone he carries and how it helped him change his life. After two weeks, the African man returns to his hometown; he writes to Lee an email requesting him to send him three gratitude stones as he is in dire need. His son suffered from a rare, incurable illness like hepatitis, and there seemed no other way. Lee sent him the three stones the African man asked for, picking those stones by the river just so they were a little special. Five months later, Lee receives an email from this man saying that his son is better and is almost healed, and they have sold over a thousand rocks for ten dollars each as gratitude rocks and raised this money for charity helping the children in need.

Gratitude, in fact, has been a universal tool used by every civilization, religion and culture to draw its benefits in every way. The powerful effects of gratitude in terms of manifesting anything that we desire holds important as the effect of gratitude on the human body is massive. To understand the effect of gratitude on our bodies, we need to first understand what role the protein immunoglobin plays in the human body.

Immunoglobin (IgA)

IgA is a protein indicator of the health of our immune system and serves as its principal defensive mechanism. IgA is a potent molecule that is one of the main proteins in maintaining a strong immune system and a strong body's natural defences. It's the polar opposite of cortisol, the stress hormone. High amounts of cortisol cause a decrease in IgA, which in turn shuts off protective genes and weakens the immune system. It's then clear to understand that the immunity of the body goes for a toss if one is living a stressful life.

In the winter of 2016, Dr Joe and his team of scientists and researchers conducted an advanced workshop in Tacoma, Washington, on the power of gratitude and other elevated feelings involving 117 participants. For each participant, their saliva samples were collected both before and after the four-day workshop study. For nine to ten minutes, three times a day, participants were asked to move into elevated emotional states, and feelings by visualizing images of love and gratitude in a meditation with their eyes closed. The results at the end of the study inspired everyone to be happier, joyful and grateful in order to live a healthy life if not for anything else.

Participants' IgA levels, on average, increased by 49.5%. There were numerous people whose IgA levels were above 100 milligrams per deciliter (mg/dl), despite the usual range being 37 to 87 mg/dl.

With their eyes closed and without any direct exposure to the outside world, the subjects had observable and profound epigenetic modifications. They were able to signal new genes to upregulate and change the genetic structure just by thinking about being in a blissful environment, and it only took a few days of experiencing positive emotions and feelings like love and joy, and that spiked their immunity beyond the normal range by igniting their genes to produce the IgA protein. Dr Joe writes in his book, concluding the research study,

"You don't need a pharmacy or an exogenous substance to heal you; you have the power to upregulate the genes that make IgA within just a few days.

Something as simple as moving into an elevated state of love, joy and gratitude for five to ten minutes a day can produce significant epigenetic changes in your health and body." ~Becoming Supernatural.

Another few research studies on gratitude were documented in the Journal of Personality and social psychology. It stated that people who kept a gratitude journal for three weeks reported better physical health and were more positive and optimistic about the future. Another research conducted at the University of California, San Diego, found that people who expressed gratitude regularly had stronger immune systems and were less likely to experience stress and depression. Oprah Winfrey, who is one of the well-known celebrities for practising and preaching gratitude, says she has benefited tremendously by keeping a gratitude journal every day, which has helped her stay more positive and focused on the blessings and the good things in life.

The brain-changing effects of gratitude

As managed health care has become more prevalent, with its emphasis on speed and brevity, mental health providers have been forced to ask themselves, "How can I assist my clients in getting the most out of therapy in the least amount of time?"

Recent research has shown that combining psychological treatment with other activities that are easy on the client yet have a high payoff may be an effective strategy. Gratitude practice is one such activity that has caught our attention in our study. It's true that several studies conducted over the last decade have shown that those who regularly practice gratitude report higher levels of happiness and very fewer instances of depression.

The issue is that the majority of studies on thankfulness have only included individuals who are otherwise successful. Do people who have mental health issues benefit from practising gratitude? And if so, what way?

The Greater Good Science Centre conducted a study with approximately 300 individuals, the vast majority of whom were college students seeking mental health therapy, to investigate these topics. Participants were recruited just before their first therapy session; on average, they indicated clinically poor levels of mental health. Depression and anxiety were common among those who sought out counselling services at this institution.

Their research participants were divided at random into three groups. All three groups received therapy, but the first group was given an additional assignment—to express gratitude to a different individual once a week for three weeks. The second group was given the opposite assignment—to express their innermost sentiments and thoughts concerning traumatic situations to another individual. Members in the third group were not assigned any written work.

I am not surprised by the results, as participants who wrote gratitude letters reported significantly better mental health for twelve weeks after the writing exercise concluded compared to those who wrote about negative experiences or received only counselling and therapy. This shows that people struggling with mental health issues might also benefit from practising gratitude through writing. In fact, it seems that the advantages of psychological therapies are amplified by the addition of a gratitude practice, even if just for a short period of time.

Not only that but also further analysis of the data revealed clues about the possible effects of gratitude on their cognitive and physiological functioning. Although more study is needed, the following four observations provide some explanations for the positive effects of gratitude on mental health. Firstly, gratitude liberates us from negative emotions. Secondly, it's beneficial to be thankful even if you don't express your appreciation. Thirdly, the positive effects of gratitude don't materialize instantly. Fourthly, the impacts of gratitude on the brain and body are long-lasting.

The Gratitude Meditation

During the pandemic, when the pharmacies sold out selling vitamin C supplements, I sold personalized gratitude meditations in abundance for the same reason. Perhaps, that's how I kept my immunity up high and barely even got close to the covid flu. This meditation is no rocket science. **Please use the open focus technique,** as discussed earlier, to start with this meditation once you close your eyes. Think about three events in your entire life that you are extremely grateful for, and visualize these three events as deeply as you can while you elevate every emotion and feeling using gratitude. At the end of all three events, place your right hand on your heart gently and give thanks wholeheartedly to the Universe or God three times for each event and open your eyes. You can use this meditation as a pocket tool whenever you feel stressed or whenever you get a sweet spot for a few minutes to sit with your eyes closed.

Superhuman and The Science of The Placebo Effect

You might have tumbled over the word "placebo" and have wondered how true would this law of belief be but never comprehended its true power. It was the same case with me for years before I had my ultimate transformation. I sat and wondered why is this science of belief so under spoken in the medical communities all these years, and that is when I comprehended the powerful marketing and implementation strategies of the pharmaceutical drug industry. In fact, throughout decades, countless experiments have been done to prove the worthiness of this one science but barely achieved any limelight. The placebo effect demonstrates the power of belief and how a strong belief can override the genetic structure of the body and compel it to heal the deadliest of diseases, almost without any surgical intervention but magic. Magic, to me, on the other hand, is something which we refer to when we don't know how it is done. But when we know how it is done, it becomes science; it becomes technology. So, let's plug out magic from this and understand the science behind it so that we can use it as technology. Another virtual tool in our pocket.

As we proceed to understand the power of placebo, we also have to understand the power of nocebo, the counter effect of placebo. If a placebo is a positive belief about healing, nocebo is a negative belief or effect. Here are a few placebo and nocebo experiments performed around the world, well documented and published in prestigious scientific journals and included in the research of these legendary scientists we have spoken about earlier in the book.

A pendulum swinging between Placebo and Nocebo

Bruno Klopfer, a psychologist, published an article in a peer-reviewed journal in 1957, telling a story of a man, Mr Wright, who suffered from advanced lymphoma, a cancer of the lymph glands. He had big tumours all around his body, almost the size of an orange. As the doctors had given up on his medical treatments and disclosed, he barely had days to live, if not a month. Being shattered, looking into the eyes of death, Wright thought to himself and said this hospital that declared his illness to be irreversible, at this point, is just one of the ten hospitals in the city, and he strongly hoped there was some magic that will heal his cancer and he developed a robust will to live. As he got to know a trial drug was out for an experiment for his precise illness, he knew this was the answer to his hope. The American medical association declared a specific drug derived from horse blood called Krebiozen. He ran to his doctor, pleading for a chance to become one of the ten people being administered this drug for the test. He was rejected as the test of this drug required the patient to have a minimum life expectancy of three months which Wright failed the prerequisite. He insisted his doctor help him off the record and administer the new drug as he knew his healing was written in this new experimental drug.

As he was administered Krebiozen by his doctor unofficially, the doctors in three days reported his orange sized tumours dissolved like snowballs on a hot stove and dissolving less than half the size. In ten days, the miracle was at rest, with Wright walking around and joking with the hospital staff exactly like a newly healed being and being discharged from the hospital. However, after two months of Wright living completely cancer free, the American medical association published an article in the media saying the ten trials conducted using Krebiozen were an utter failure. Wright, with shock absorbing the news and embracing the fact that the news was right, relapsed in no time. When Wright's doctor Dr Philip intervened in his relapse, he realized that Wrights's previous healing could be of the placebo effect and observing his patient to be terminally ill and there was not much to lose, he put his analysis to use. Dr Philip made up a story saying that the American medical association later disclosed that the ten trials were done from a batch that was defective and that a new advanced version of the drug is on the way, which is twice more powerful as the one before. Mr Wright was asked to come back the next day to take his new drug shot on priority. Dr Philip loaded his injection with distilled water and administered it to Wright with confidence on his face.

Write healed the same way as earlier, and in just a few days, he was discharged from the hospital totally cancer free. Dr Philips's theory proved it right. It was the placebo that healed Mr Wright, and it is no magic. He lived healthy and happy for two months till one day, the American medical association published in the media that the drug Krebiozen was a fake drug that contained only some amino acid mineral oil, and the company that manufactured this drug was sued in the American court of law. After hearing this news, Wright relapsed for the last time, losing all his hope for healing. He was hospitalized, and he died in two days. The question is, what caused this pendulum to swing between placebo and nocebo effect? It was the belief Wright held strong in his mind to heal and, sadly, to die too. His body was capable of simply melting away his tumours and was also capable of recreating his disease "twice," ultimately taking him to his deathbed.

Experimental Placebo Surgeries

In 1996, Bruce Mosley, an orthopaedic surgeon at the Baylor College of Medicine and one of the leading experts in the field of orthopaedic sports medicine, published an experimental study on ten volunteers suffering from severe osteoarthritis of the knee. Because of the severity of the illness, these men were barely able to walk unassisted. Dr Mosley divided the patients into two groups. The first group received proper surgery involving anaesthesia, cutting two slits and scraping the affected and degenerated cartilage out of the knee and stitching the two slits. The first group performed the entire surgery involving the needed procedure, and the second group was administered a fake surgery. The second group of patients got their knees anaesthetized, made two slits, and simply stitched back like the normal surgical procedure. After the surgery, it was noted that both groups experienced healing and less pain. The patients were asked to come for a follow-up after six months, and the results were the same; also, after six years, when they were followed up, all ten patients were living pain-free and full of joy. Inspired by this study and research, Dr Mosley conducted another similar experiment involving 180 patients suffering from osteoarthritis. The same was the results for both the groups in this experiment when the team followed up after two years.

Another example of a placebo surgery experiment was documented in the 1950s. This experiment involved patients who suffered a heart attack and were due a surgery called inter mammary ligation, which involved tying up the affected arteries (this is much before the present bypass graft surgery). The group patients were again divided into two, and the first group received a real surgery (slitting the chest and tying the affected arteries and stitching back), and the second group received a fake surgery (just slitting and stitching back). The results amazed the doctors and scientists onboard this experiment. 67% of the group that received the actual surgery reported relief and less pain, whereas 83% of the fake surgery patients reported relief and less pain. Realizing the placebo surgery was more effective than the actual procedure startled the team. Kept them wondering, the power of the human mind!

Another research experiment was performed in Japan in the 1960s for the Nocebo effect. A group of thirteen children who were all severely allergic to poison Ivy were chosen. The research scientists took a simple leaf and rubbed it on the forearm of each child, saying it was a poison Ivy leaf, and took a real poison Ivy leaf and rubbed it on the other forearm and saying to the children it was a simple normal leaf. It was noticed that the arm that was rubbed with simple leaf developed rashes and swelling, whereas the arm that was rubbed with poison Ivy leaf reported no rash or reaction at all. In fact, eleven children out of thirteen did not have any reaction to the actual poison Ivy leaf.

There are no incurable diseases, but incurable patients.

~ Dr Bernie Siegel

If "the placebo effect" is about the belief we have about someone or something outside of us (e.g. the doctor, surgery or medicine), then it wouldn't be wrong to say we can build a specific belief by being conscious or using therapy and create the same effects in our biology as these research experiments have proven. Author Norman

Cousins writes in his book, Anatomy of Illness.

"The placebo proves that there is no real separation between mind and body. Illness is always an interaction between both. It can begin in the mind and affect the body, or it can begin in the body and affect the mind. He also mentions attempts to treat most mental diseases as though they were completely free of physical causes and attempts to cure most bodily diseases as though the mind was nowhere involved must be considered archaic in the light of the new evidence about the way the human body functions; the drug is not always necessary for healing, belief in recovery always is."

Chapter - 5

What Is Meditation

We have all heard about this one word, "meditation," all around, but not many understand what it really means. Before my phase of transformation, I knew there was no cure for cancer or diabetes, but I also knew meditation has helped many around the world get rid of their irreversible ailments. I very well also knew that meditation would bring immense peace and happiness into one's life if practised dedicatedly. Knowing all this was never a first-hand or even a second-hand experience to me and always kept me ignorant of this one powerful tool till one day, a close loved one almost lost her life, carelessly practising a master-level meditation ritual without any guidance. As you know, if you go to the gym on day one and attempt a hundred kg deadlift, you are bound to tear your back muscles. This innocent girl found a powerful guided meditation on YouTube, which was to awaken and raise a very powerful dormant energy from the base of the spine all the way up to the brain. She performed this meditation for nothing more than three days without knowing these super advanced master-level meditations need years of dedicated and guided practice before reaching a phase of performing them. The result was she hit herself with a psychosis attack. Her brain and body, which were incapable of hosting such highly powerful energies, got thrown out of balance, and she had to be admitted to a psychiatric hospital for close to a month and got administered brain shocks (ECT) to numb the prefrontal part of her brain. She became delusional, schizophrenic and suicidal, and she could barely have any distinction between her physical, mental and spiritual reality. As all this happened for the first time in my life, first hand, encountering the adverse effect of doing a meditation in the wrong way, I had no choice but to force myself to look deeper into this much-ignored word meditation. I understood this much if doing a meditation in the wrong way could harm someone to hell, doing it the right way can open doors to paradise.

Many of the world's oldest religions, cultures and societies used meditation as means to connect with the divine and achieve an elevated state of mind and consciousness. Preserving one's physical, mental and spiritual well-being via a variety of meditation rituals dates back thousands of years.

As a practice, meditation has long been a way to channel our life force to bring about a more positive and fruitful future in terms of health, wealth, and success. Every day, our bodies generate an incredible amount of electromagnetic energy, which we may direct toward the goals of our choice. However, focusing on material items or events drains our vitality because of the unseen emotional connection we establish with each one of them. Meditating may refocus our energy and utilize it for the greater good. By understanding that one's focus determines the direction of one's energy flow, we can unplug the invisible chords that drain our energy reserves.

Imagine how much energy we waste subconsciously, given that contemporary research suggests that individuals have anywhere from sixty to a hundred thoughts every minute about all the many people, things, locations, circumstances and events in their lives. While we do meditation as a daily practice, the number of thoughts that go through our heads decreases with time, allowing us more control over where we direct our focus and energy.

This repetitive mental and emotional misery keeps us in a state of high stress and worry, reducing our quality of life to that of a survival mechanism. When our lives depend on it, we default to a purely materialist perspective based on what we can see via our five senses: sight, sound, smell, and taste. Stress hormones like cortisol and adrenaline make us focus only on the external environment pin pointedly, where threats are most likely to be found and compromise the immunity of our body.

The human body's "fight or flight" reaction is among the primitive and most basic survival mechanisms. Naturally, when it first evolved into our system, its reaction was beneficial. It adapted to our needs and helped us survive. Now, however, in the twenty-first century, such is obviously not the case. We lose a lot of our creative energy, infuse our bodies with enormous amounts of cortisol, and drastically reduce our immunity after just one phone call or email from our boss or family member that ignites a strong emotional response like anger, frustration, fear, anxiety, sadness, guilt, suffering, or shame, and this causes us to emotionally react as if a predator is chasing us.

If you understand that your thoughts and emotions are constantly producing an electromagnetic field as a result of your mental and emotional attachments to a variety of external events, then you must also believe that you are producing a future nothing but identical to your past.

You may free yourself from your bad emotions and build a life that isn't bound by your past if you can free your focus from the unwanted things in your external environment. That's why meditation should be a common practice for shifting our focus towards what is needed.

By shifting your focus within, you begin to release your emotional and energetic ties to the external world and make room for creating a new future.

Here are a few meditation-related titbits you may have heard before (I could not believe them until I tried them myself):

1. Being a mediator will make you happy

A recent study found that meditators report much higher levels of happiness than nonmeditators. It is well-known that the practice of meditation may increase the rate at which good ideas and feelings flood one's mind. Regular meditation, even for only a few minutes, has profound effects, as we have learnt in the earlier chapters in the many experiments performed around the world. Several scientific investigations on meditating Monks, Yogis and Sufis provide enough scientific proof for this assertion. How does it make you a happier person? With time you become conscious of all of your negative emotions and beliefs in your mind, and you will be in a place to consciously choose happiness over the misery that was earlier out of your control. Before I started my journey being a meditator, if someone cut me off while I was driving, I would cuss and fuss and deplete a big chunk of my energy for no reason. After embarking on this journey of meditativeness, I found myself to be conscious of not writing a big check of energy to just some random driver who cut me off; rather, I became capable of giving thought to why someone is driving in a hurry, maybe he or she is rushing to the hospital or maybe anything. I now would bless the one in a hurry to be safe. As the great Indian mystic says, what happens outside of you is not in your control, but what happens inside of you should definitely be in your control.

2. Anxiety, tension, and sadness are all alleviated via regular meditation practice

Simplifying meditation, imagine driving down from work late evening and getting stuck in downtown traffic with countless cars and how wretched you feel; now imagine taking off from your local airport and seeing the same traffic from five thousand feet above. How beautiful does the traffic look from above? How do the street lights and the vehicle lights look? Your perception about the same thing feels poles apart. That's the difference meditation creates between you and your anxieties. It creates a conscious gap between you and your life events so that you can take a distant view of your anxieties and consciously stay detached from what is necessary. The power of meditation to change one's life is something that shouldn't be discounted. Researchers at the University of Wisconsin found that meditating really changes the brain's chemistry. Studies have shown, for instance, that regular meditation practice may lead to a reduction in the size of the region of the brain responsible for stress and anxiety. Meditators teach their minds to be resilient in the face of adversity by focusing on the present moment. There is also a notable reduction in the amount of worry people feel as a result of future events. I was a very anxious person before marching on this journey, but now I gained the capability to choose if I have to be anxious about something upcoming or be a conscious creator and create that short upcoming as I desire it to be. I am also conscious enough to choose gratitude over sadness. Rather than feeling sad, I found the capability to see what I am blessed with and be grateful for that.

3. In order to benefit from meditation, you do not need to be religious

Professional Meditation practitioners are certain that everyone can get something from meditation, while being a theist or an atheist. Even though meditation is an integral part of many faith traditions, it is not required to engage in any contemplation when taking a scientific approach. Science has evolved to a point where it plays in the same arena as spirituality, and the quantum field, as we learnt in the earlier chapters, is the present moment all have spoken about. It is a field of spiritual engagement where we tap into and create what we desire.

4. The positive effects of meditation are felt nearly immediately

There are many positive effects of meditation on one's health, which is yet another compelling argument for taking up the practice. Some positive effects of simply sitting with eyes closed might become immediately apparent. Even if it's brief and understated, most people have experienced a sense of tranquillity and peace of mind at some point. Lawyer Jeana Cho listed six unexpected advantages, including a decrease in unconscious prejudice based on age and ethnicity, in a recent online Forbes article. The busyness of one's thoughts may lead some meditators to think that their practice has the opposite impact, always taking them off course. Please don't give up on it, and remember to keep your sessions brief when you start. When you meditate, you don't try to erase whatever thoughts pop into your head; instead, you learn to accept them as they are and become more attuned to them. It's not that the thoughts in your head simply disappear. When you are meditative, you are conscious of not giving any emotional response to negative thoughts, and then those thoughts will simply dissolve. You're already one step ahead of the game if you've realized how chaotic and draining unnecessary mental activity can be.

5. Sleep better, thanks to meditation

Everyone worries about having an insomniac night at some point. Unfortunately, almost one-third of the American population experiences sleep loss on a regular basis. Meditation might help you sleep if you're one of the unfortunate people who can't seem to fall asleep by staring at the ceiling or counting sheep. Some people experience the opposite problem: they fall asleep as soon as they begin meditating. This is confirmed by an article in the Harvard Health Blog.

6. Focus is enhanced by meditation

Meditation not only improves your mood and quality of life, but it also aids with cognitive functions by establishing a razor-sharp focus. By practising meditation, one learns to pay attention to their immediate surroundings without passing judgment or reaching conclusions. As a result, you'll be less easily carried away by distractions. A very successful businessman in the United States who scaled his business unrealistically high in a very less amount of time came under the surveillance of the local authorities. As his business was interrogated, the authorities found no malpractice responsible for the humungous growth this young businessman achieved. When he was asked about how he made it happen, he said, "I can keep my focus on one thing for more than twenty seconds which none of you is capable of, and that is what makes my business super successful". An average human mind is capable of having a conscious focus for nothing more than two to eight seconds, and that's what makes all our tasks more difficult.

7. It is the most powerful manifestation tool

As we have learnt what affirmations are, how journaling helps, how positive thinking and being grateful helps and how helpful visualizations are in order to manifest what we desire, nothing can still be as powerful as meditation. As the core of meditation is tapping into the present moment or the quantum field, which is going beyond our logical and thinking mind and experiencing a moment of trance, that is where creation and manifestation take form. If all the above titbits don't inspire you enough to come on board this journey, surely manifesting your favourite car, your dream house, your dream job, your perfect partner, or abundance of wealth, all are a thousand per cent possibility if you surrender to this one tool with dedication.

Being in the Present Moment

The roller coaster ride that in life is never smooth. All of us, at one time or another, go through hard situations. In a nutshell, this is how it is. However, it is essential that we not allow ourselves to get paralyzed by fear or to allow ourselves to become a continuous source of concern over things that can be avoided. The stress hormone cortisol is increased in the body when stress and worry are present on a continuous basis. Living in this condition simply promotes our body's ability to utilize our hard-earned muscle for energy and to store fat more effectively. In addition to weakening our resistance to disease, we learnt earlier that long-term stress totally has a negative impact on our immune system. The detrimental effects of stress, anxiety, and other unpleasant emotions on our health are clear and undeniable, and we understand that stress and damaging beliefs combined are well capable of costing someone their life.

Having experienced the difficulties of divorce, suicidal traumas, major financial setbacks, mental sickness, and other losses, I have discovered that living in the now is one of the most helpful ways to cope with adversity. We tend to dwell on the past or worry about the future much too much. But if we detach consciously from the past and the future, we won't have anything to worry about in the present, right?

The greatest way to cope with grief, stress, worry, regret, and anxiety is to take things one day (or one moment) at a time. I understand this is not simple, but surely adding psychotherapeutic assistance will greatly help with regular meditation.

The challenge is to not allow these things to rule our lives to the point that we are overtaken by anxiety and stress that might harm our health, but they are all valid causes for feeling out of sorts. The answer lies in the realization that each of us can consciously decide and choose how to respond to adversity or, in fact, any event in life.

For instance, whether consciously or unconsciously, we make the decision to be anxious. Since anxiety is a condition that occurs when we are preoccupied with the future or the past, focusing on the here and now helps us shift from worrying to just being. This is of utmost significance when coping with events outside our control. If you pause right now, you have the option of choosing to be at peace with whatever is troubling you. A good pause can be referred to as a simple five-minute fourfold breath transcendental meditation technique, as mentioned in the earlier chapters.

Oh, I get it; that's easier said than done. In the same way that I discovered that focusing on the here and now was helpful in getting me through some tough times in my life, I also picked up some useful techniques for cultivating mindfulness.

The law of your inner world is stillness, and the law of your outer world is dynamism.

This happened decades ago when I was working in the aviation industry. Flying on aeroplanes that were almost airborne for six days straight a week troubled me thinking about aviation safety. Especially when these aircraft, as I noticed, have been flying for over two decades and still have the certified airworthiness to commercially fly passengers from one point to another with flight times exceeding ten to twelve hours straight. This compelled me to question the aircraft maintenance engineers how are these machines that are more than twenty years old are still considered safe to fly. The answer was nothing too technical that I got. The AME replied, saying if the aircraft was to be more on the ground, it wouldn't survive a decade of airworthiness, but because it was more in the air than on the ground, it is still in a condition to fly and transport passengers as the aircraft was designed to be in the air than to be on the ground. It also made me realize if I had to park my car in my garage for years without taking it out on a drive frequently, the mechanism of my car would deteriorate in its ways and would no longer abide by passenger and road safety.

As the law of dynamism states continuous motion, it is evident to understand that if we have to keep our fleshy machinery at its peak performance, it has to be in motion; it has to move. As hilarious as it may sound, humans are not trees; they flourish and evolve when they move, exercise and travel.

Exercise is an excellent way to focus on the here and now (if you don't have trekking a mountain as an option). Kickboxing, CrossFit, or even Zumba are all great options. But if you don't like these courses, going to the gym and lifting weights is a terrific way to focus on the here and now as well. Try to choose an exercise routine that is just difficult enough to keep you focused. After indulging in regular physical exercise, you will not only feel good about yourself, but you will also see the physical benefits. This also makes us understand the epigenetic research study of slightly heavy men who upregulated 7000 genes for health and vitality just by aerobics alone.

When we have a clear goal in mind, no matter what kind of activity or exercise we're doing, we tend to lose track of time and enjoy the experience more than we otherwise would. We can't think about the past or the future if we live in the present moment. To put it simply, I think you should exercise or take a class to push yourself and work toward some modest objectives. Exercising is a great way to relieve tension and forget about your problems for a while. In addition, your body will be flooded with "feel-good" endorphins after you finish your exercise. Furthermore, all your hard work at the gym would have left you feeling fantastic physically, which is known to have a beneficial effect on your mood.

There are various ways to meditate, but concentrating on the empty space around your body and breathing is usually the quickest and most effective. "Mindful meditation" is another term for this kind of concentration. The act of breathing is one of the few bodily functions that are autonomous and completely under our control. Thankfully, breathing occurs even when we don't give it much thought, and it's also possible to breathe normally while doing other things. Concentrated breathing is a powerful tool for relieving tension and anxiety. Also, paying attention to our breathing and concentrating on each inhalation and exhalation is a great way to kick off a meditation practice.

In addition to soothing the central nervous system, deep, quiet, and deliberate breathing meditations have been demonstrated to relax the whole body (which can be over-activated from chronic anxiety and stress). During meditation, the parasympathetic nervous system in the ANS is activated, which repairs any damage caused by stress and returns the body to normal functioning. Reducing stress via meditation has additional benefits, including physiological ones like decreased cortisol and blood pressure, as well as psychological ones like improved immunological response and clarity of thought.

In the beginning, meditation may seem strange and challenging; it takes work to get used to it. Concentration training, like physical exercise or cycling, has the effect of making the skill more automatic with practice. The ability to keep one's mind on a single task for an extended period of time is indicative of growth. Even if you can just meditate for fifteen minutes a day, you should make the time since the advantages to your body and mind are enormous.

Chanting And Recitations and Their Power to Harness Energies

It doesn't matter which religion you belong to; every religion has been passed down, sustaining for thousands of years its practice and purpose to help the human race achieve its highest potential. Lies, propaganda and meaningless texts dissolve in a period of a few hundred years, but truth has the lawful capability to survive and get passed down for generations and generations to come. Every chant and verse preached by various religions or cultures evolved from sacred mathematics and the law of vibrations. These chants and verses hold powerful effects on the human body if performed in specific vibrational ways. Some of these chants and verses have the power to pierce through into the quantum field of our nonphysical world. Also, some of these ancient words, letters and texts are vibrationally designed to impact the physical world in ways to trigger healing or manifest what you desire.

SHUMANNS RESONANCE: The Earth's heartbeat

In the 1960s, W.O. Schumann, a German scientist, coined a term known as Schumann's resonance, underlining an electromagnetic phenomenon that occurs between Earth's surface and the ionosphere. This electromagnetic activity is our planet's aura or the energy field. Similar to the electromagnetic field of the human body, planet Earth has its electromagnetic signature field. This field was extensively researched and studied in the 1960s and concluded the hypothesis claiming the planetary energy field to be 7.83 hertz, predating as far as thousands of years. The planetary energy field has been of great importance to every civilization and religion as it was preached to be the closest frequency to God. It is not of any surprise that the human brain tunes into this frequency during the states of sleep or theta brain waves, as we learnt earlier.

If you have heard about the scientific phenomenon called Geo-magnetism, it is most commonly used by birds and animals to navigate long distances. Have you wondered how birds can fly across continents without a single direction? Knowing that one degree of angle shift in the flight path can lead a bird or even an aeroplane thousands of miles off its course. It is because a bird's brain, in its state of wakefulness, is in tune with the planetary vibration of 7.8hz and hence making it possible to access the geo-magnetism phenomenon and navigate straight to their point of destination.

This leads to a question, why are we as human beings depend on GPS for navigating our travel? If the birds can do it, what stops us from using the geomagnetic phenomenon? It is simple; the human brain is highly evolved, and it is not wrong to say it evolved higher than the pace of planetary evolution itself. That is what makes humans to be cognitive beings, able to communicate using language or read or write. As we learnt in the earlier chapters, the beta brain wave is what makes verbal communication possible in the human brain, and the brains of most of the other species have not evolved beyond theta (4-8hz trance states).

The human brain being highly evolved should have been a blessing but has turned into a curse because we fail to access the planetary frequency of 7.8hz in our states of wakefulness. The moment our brains tune into theta, our five physical faculties go to rest, thus being of barely any use when we are awake. The reason a lot of people have their intuitions at their peak during dreamy sleep states is that when dreaming, we are tuned into a field of information that is infinite and well connected to that of our planet, a field that is a part of the quantum field itself.

Many religions and cultures have found ways of tuning into this energy field using the arts of chanting and recitations. Looking at the world's three biggest religions in the modern age and their sciences pointing towards the significance of their sacred texts involves the frequency of 7.8hz.

Aaum, Aameen & Aamenn

The above three sacred words, when demystified, reveal the glory of the frequency 7.8hz. Depending on which word you connect to, you can effectively use its vibration towards the end of praying for your desires, be it to manifest healing or a perfect partner or a dream job. Meditating simply on any of the sacred texts mentioned above can help you benefit from its science miraculously. It is said and personally experienced that just chanting and reciting either of the three you connect to is enough to untie you from every misery that can be created by mankind. If the open focus technique or any breathing technique is difficult for you to practice, simply chanting any of these three words in repetition before and after a strong visualization can bring the lot you desire to live.

Chanting and recitations are vibrational rituals, not only vocal

As much as chanting or recitations soothe our ears, the purpose of it is vibrational in nature. The human body has three main vibration points, one in the gut region, the second in the heart-to-throat region and the third in the head region. Chanting vibrationally refers to these three points in synchronized vibration in accordance with the sacred texts. For example, when chanting AA-U-MM or AAMMEEN or AAAMENN, the first point of vibration is to be sensed in the gut, then taking the vibration upward towards the throat region and ends in the head. Though chanting and recitations take some practice before becoming vibrationally powerful in your system, it is always good to start today.

What is Personalized Meditation?

Have you ever thought less than thrice before taking any medications consulting the famous Google doctor? Yes, we prefer consulting a certified physician and taking a personalized prescription. It is wise to understand that the physician, after consulting, personalizes a series of medications necessary for your recovery, some medications are high in the dose, and some are low, depending upon the diagnosis, and that is what leaves an impact on your healing and recovery; it is the balanced, personalized prescription. At ARF Healing Scope, we look at meditations as crucial as medications and believe in the impact of creating the right prescription as needed. However, for the sake of this book and the readers, I have written down the most important points involved in the process of designing your personalized meditation and recording it on your phone's voice recording app to begin with your meditation journey. The meditation script mentioned towards the end of the book is just to manifest what you desire. Still, if you are seeking your ultimate healing or your ultimate transformation, I would advise you to connect with our team to design your detailed personalized meditation and run the necessary therapies that are needed on your journey to becoming superhuman.

How to Combine NLP and Personalized Transcendental Meditation to Create the Life You Want

As I designed this program almost five years back, initially, it used to take close to two hours every day for twenty-five days to deliver this program from the start to the end. When I combined NLP with embrace the superhuman, I can now wind up this program in just five days. Why am I expressing this, transcendental meditations for manifestations are powerful, but as we learnt earlier, if our subconscious mind holds any pattern against what we desire, our manifestation would take way more time to hit reality if not a failure. Because for a fact, if I want to manifest a career where I desire to get a pay check of 100,000 dollars every month, I will have to first change every belief stored in my subconscious mind that says I can never make that amount of money in a month. Even if my subconscious mind has negative emotions that say I am worthless or have been mocked down throughout my childhood and that I cannot achieve anything in life, these emotions will never let me create what I desire.

As the subconscious mind is the chief editor for every feeling that we create, it will take way longer time to reprogram the subconscious mind using the repetition technique and then clear out our path towards vibrating the right electromagnetic energy in the quantum field. With the help of NLP therapies, as we understood earlier, its merely magic to uninstall any negative emotion or change any damaging belief. That is why underlining what you desire to manifest is the first part; the second part is to intervene if there are any negative emotions or damaging beliefs against what you want to manifest. For healing negative emotions and damaging beliefs, you can best connect to our team of therapists and coaches at www.arfhealingscope.com.

Once you declutter your mind from all that is negative and damaging, manifesting anything you desire will be a cakewalk. The electromagnetic impulse you create with a cluttered mind will be a very weak one in comparison to a healed or reprogrammed mind.

The personalized meditation module

Once you are in the sweet spot of the generous present moment, where you can tune into the infinite possibilities for your future, you need two things: a clear thought and an elevated feeling. Your clear thought is exactly what you understood: you need to be clear about what you want to manifest and describe it in detail. Let's say you want to buy your dream house; you have to be clear in visualizing and feeling every detail of your house, from how it looks from the outside, to how the main door looks like, to the interiors, the colour of the walls, the design of the chandeliers, type of curtains, to the furniture in the house, every detail must be felt deeply when you linger in the quantum field or the present moment. Blending the energy of gratitude after visualizing and feeling the details will help to a great extent in creating more powerful energy impulses in the quantum field. "Feeling all these details as if it has already happened" is the key to effective manifestations.

When you have to combine that thought with an elevated feeling like gratitude, inspiration, joy, excitement, awe, wonder, etc., you will have to tap into the feelings you feel when your thought comes true and then feel the emotion before your desire actually manifests. The electromagnetic charge you send into the field is your high energy, the elevated feeling your heart generates. As you already know, when you combine the electrical charge (your thought) with the magnetic charge (elevated feeling) for twenty-one days, you create a higher electromagnetic signature field that is the same as your state of being.

Do you understand? Make it as clear and detailed as you can, and assign a letter or two or maybe three as a symbol to all you desire to manifest in this field of infinite possibilities. As you learn that your thoughts and feelings are the electrical and magnetic charge you send out into the quantum field, you will be able to use this knowledge to your highest advantage.

This makes sense because the new electromagnetic signal you send out would attract waves and frequencies in the field that are a vibrational match.

When your energy and the energy of your desired manifestation match in vibration, the longer you are aware of that energy, the easier you attract and magnetize that experience to you.

As we learnt, if you do it as a victim, someone who's suffering, or someone who feels limited and unhappy, your energy will never match up with what you desire to manifest because the vibration of your victimization and the vibration of what you desire to manifest will be completely different from each other.

Strong elevated feelings play a big role in the process because they are one of the most powerful ways to attract matter. You know that feeling that you get which feels like an explosion in your chest, and you feel that vibration in your hands? You probably might have felt that when you saw your child when he or she was born or when you got a big promotion in life, or when you handed over a hundred dollars to a homeless man because he has not eaten in days. I am talking about just that feeling, that energy explosion you might have felt throughout your body, and it made you feel blissed out and content and happy; that type of feeling is what we need to create as frequently as possible. Most of the sacred chants are designed to create an explosive electromagnetic field.

René Peoch's 'The Great Experiment'

It was in 1986 when a French scientist by the name of Rene Peoch demonstrated the power of emotion, feeling and desire in an experiment using baby chickens. The instinct of most birds and chickens is that when they hatch out of an egg, they believe the first moving object around them to be their mother, and they imprint on the movement of the object around them and follow it where ever it goes. For example, if the baby chicks hatch in front of you, and not the mother hen, they immediately form a belief in their mind and emotionally get attached to you and desire to be close to you, and where ever you go, they follow. As simple to understand, this is an instinct they are born with.

Rene built a robot on a technology called a random electronic generator (REG). This means this robot is designed to move randomly (50% towards the right and 50% towards the left), like the little battery-operated toy robots we played with as children. He installed a pen beneath the robot to track its movement in a special arena floored with white paper.

The experiment began when Rene placed the robot in the arena with newly hatched baby chicks who imprinted on the REG robot as their mother, and they began to follow it all around the arena. After recording the random movement of the robot with baby chicks in the arena, Rene removed all the imprinted baby chicks from the arena and placed them in a cage outside.

The astonishing research claimed its purpose when Rene recorded the movement of the robot alone in the arena to randomly move towards the side where the baby chicks were placed in a cage. What this research experiment successfully concluded was the movement of the robot was all around when the baby chicks were inside the arena and when the chicks were placed outside in a cage, their belief that the robot was their mother and the desire to be close, kept the robot moving only towards the side of the arena that was close to the cage outside and not all around the arena as it happened in the first part of the experiment.

This demonstrated the power of belief, emotion and desire to influence a "mechanical" robot's movement. As much as the limelight this research study gained in the scientific communities in 1986, it was criticized as this experiment did not fit into the Newtonian laws of physics. Rene, to prove further his research in 1995, conducted another experiment and took it a little further, using the same REG robot in the same arena. This time Rene used baby chicks that were not hatched in front of the robot and did not imprint on its movement. Again, another instinct of chickens is, they do not want to be in a dark place during day time and would desire to be in a well-lit place.

Rene performed this experiment in a dark room, placing a candle on the small REG robot. He placed all the non-imprinted chickens in a cage outside the arena and began recording the movement of the robot. As the nonimprinted chicken desired to be close to any source of light, the robot with a candle on top of it again moved randomly only towards the side of the arena where the chickens were placed in a cage.

He then took this experiment to another level; he took a rabbit this time, placed it in the arena where the robot was and recorded its movement with the pen installed underneath it. It was unexpected to witness what happened. The rabbit, initially scared of the robot, made the robot move randomly to the opposite side of the arena, where the rabbit sat frightened. Rene did not conclude the experiment at this point and waited a little longer till the rabbit became comfortable (realizing it was safe) with the presence of the robot in the arena and built a playful desire to be around the robot now. The movement of the robot changed, and now it moved closer to the side where the rabbit was. This amazing piece of research was documented in many scientific journals, and it makes us understand the power of belief, emotion, desire and fear.

Let this sink in, and I invite you to imagine how we actually control everything physically that we desire and fear even if it is not in our awareness. If we truly believe and emotionally feel what we desire as firmly as these baby chicks, we can gravitate all that we want to manifest towards us in line with the laws of "quantum physics".

Designing Your Personalised Meditation

Script The Meditation By Writing It Down.

For this meditation, you need to do a little work ahead of time. Keep in mind that the experience you desire to manifest already exists as energy or frequency in the quantum field of infinite possibilities, just like waves exist before they collapse into the matter. With this meditation, you are going to tune into this energy.

Many people around the world have lowered their cholesterol levels by tapping into this potential. They got rid of the signs of cancer. They made tumours go away and gave people new jobs, free vacations, healthy new relationships, more money, deep spiritual experiences, and even won them the lottery.

Once you've chosen the new experience you want, give it a capital letter or two and write it down in your handwriting on real paper with a real pen or pencil. This letter is a symbol of that particular possibility in your life. Actually, putting it down on paper is important, as the act of writing it down solidifies that you want it; in fact, when you write it, it is the first sign of your desire already in the physical world and no more just a thought or feeling. Then, draw two wavy circles around the letter to show the electromagnetic field you need to make around your body to match the potential in the quantum field. Write "thought" at the top of the left column and "feeling" at the top of the right column.

Now, give that letter or two you have chosen a meaning so you can understand what it means.

Thought and intention:

List a few points on what your thoughts and intentions are about achieving a new potential for your future, like for a new higher paid and better job; your thought column may look like this,

- I am making 100,000 dollars a month
- I have a big lavish office in a commercial skyscraper
- I have a big team of professionals reporting to me
- I am leaving a profound impact on all my clients and colleague's lives
- I am travelling all around the world for business and pleasure

Elevated Feelings:

Now on the left side, where the column reads "Elevated feelings," write the feelings you want to feel when you manifest this potential. You may write,

- Extremely Grateful for all this to be a part of my life

- Overjoyed with so many blessings in my life

- Awed by feeling how everyone looked up to me

- The freedom to work in your comfort

- In love with every bit of your life

- Worthy of every bit of your achievement

These are just a few examples of what your list may look like. Depending on what you desire to manifest in your life, choose your thoughts and feelings wisely. The next step is combining these two columns into a beautiful video in your mind. This is how I would combine these two columns if I desire to manifest these. Starting my meditation with the open focus technique to get my brainwaves into theta or the quantum field, I will then proceed towards visualizing the below script,

"I am walking into the lobby of my office, the receptionist welcomes me with a big smile, and I walk towards the elevator and see a few of my staff waiting there. They greet me with so much love and gratitude for making them a part of my company. As I look at each one's face, I feel awed and so grateful that I keep my hand on my heart and thank God or the universe for this wonderful blessing. I get off the elevator and walk into my big lavish office, noticing every detail, from the staff cubicles to the beautiful pantry and cafeteria, my huge office cabin. I notice every corner of my cabin and feel so grateful and in love with my dream job that I feel this beautiful high energy rush up and down my body from head to toe. This feeling is so amazing and is such a blessing.

It is the first of the month, and my company has paid me my first check of $100,000. Holding that in my hand, I feel so successful and overjoyed with my achievement. I call my wife and share this wonderful news with excitement and joy. I feel so worthy at this moment that I deserve every bit of this success.

I am flying on a business class seat to a foreign destination that I desired to visit for a long time. I feel so financially abundant that all these luxuries are now a part of me and my life. I am so much in love with every bit of my life."

The script can go on as deep and detailed as it can, and I am sure you got an idea of how your visualization may look and how your heart will feel while you visualize and meditate on your script. I encourage you to add anything and everything that may make your heart vibrate and feel over the skies. As we learnt earlier, "the stronger the feeling, the higher the impact."

The best way to record your meditation is on your phone's voice recorder app in your voice; blending some soothing instrumental music in the background will be great. Recording it slowly using the mentioned time gaps will be highly beneficial.

Once you start on your journey of meditativeness and manifestation, I recommend you choose three different things that you like to manifest, to begin with, as three is a good number. Once you have written down a script for three things you desire to manifest in the above format, please visit our company website arfhealingscope.com to perform a free one-time simple guided meditation therapy kit which is designed specifically to prime and program your mind in the necessary ways needed for creating an instant impact on your personalized meditation ritual. These meditation therapies in the kit cleanse your mind from any limiting beliefs, negative emotions, disempowered feelings and feeling of non-worthiness toward the three things you desire to manifest.

The meditation script-

Take a deep and comfortable breath, and as you exhale, close your eyes.

(5sec)

Relax every muscle in your body from head to toe.

(10sec)

Breathe fresh air and oxygen into every muscle of your body.

(10sec)

Become aware of the empty space around your head.

(5sec)

Become aware of the empty space in front of your eyes.

(5sec)

Become aware of the empty space behind your head.

(5sec)

Become aware of the empty space around every part of your body.

(10sec)

Become aware of the empty space around you in the room.

(10sec)

Float up and above your body, seeing yourself sitting down where you are.

(5sec)

Float up and above that, so you can see your house from above.

(5sec)

Float above the clouds and float into space.

(5sec)

Float above our solar system and out into deep space.

(5sec)

Become aware of the eternal blackness of deep space.

(5sec)

You see the number five, big and bright in the eternal darkness

(5sec)

You see the number slowly become dim and disappear slowly

(5sec)

You see number four, big and bright in eternal darkness

(5sec)

You see the number four dissolve and disappear

(5sec)

You see number three, big and bright in the eternal darkness

(5sec)

You see this number dissolve and disappear slowly

(5sec)

You see number two, big and bright

(5sec)

You see this number dissolve into an eternity of darkness

(5sec)

You are seeing number one, big and bright

(5sec)

You see this number dissolve and disappear in this eternity of blackness

(5sec)

Become aware of sensing nothing physical in deep space.

(5sec)

Become aware that you are not your body, and none of your senses (5sec)

Become aware of nothingness.

(5sec)

Say to yourself eleven times as you inhale, "I am not my mind," and as you exhale, "I am not even my body."

(30sec)

Now think about the letters you have assigned to the desired manifestation.

Think about every intention you had set for this letter that you want to manifest.

(5sec)

Know that all these thoughts and desires already exist at this moment.

(5sec)

PASTE YOUR VISUAL SCRIPT HERE

(5sec)

Feel every bit of that beautiful life.

(5sec)

Feel how your heart is at ease and pulsing with blissful energy.

(5sec)

Feel that vibration in your chest.

What you are feeling in your body right now is your new electromagnetic signature, and this feeling is what will attract your desired future in your life.

Finally, surrender to the present moment.

(5sec)

Give gratitude and be thankful.

Surrender to the infinite possibilities of potential in the present moment; be thankful with all your heart.

(5sec)

Bless your soul, bless your past, and bless your future.

Bless the divine in you, open your heart, and give thanks for a new life before it is made to manifest.

(5sec)

Float down to earth from deep space, like a rocket, and float down through the clouds, then float down into your room and your body.

(5sec)

Become aware of the empty space in the room, and when you are ready, take a deep breath in and as you exhale, open your eyes.

Get up from meditation as though your future has already happened, and let the synchronicities and new possibilities find you.

———— ◆ ————

Epilogue

This book has been written with a deep intention of helping every one tap in to their highest potential and live a happy, content and a healed life. As the philosophers, saints and sages have said, the highest version of you unveils with tremendous pain, made me realize my journey of pain towards my ultimate transformation. My heart still aches for the ones walking this path of reincarnating a new self in the old body with pain and misery. You know when you endured the deepest of pains, and walked out of hell burning the old self into ashes, your heart, your soul becomes just love and the deepest empathy that evoked with in you will never want another to suffer the way you have suffered. Yes, this was my journey as some of you, and for this vary reason I dedicated my life towards decoding what shifted in my biology and physiology during the most dreadful yet the most powerful experience of my life "The dark night of the soul". With this experience and knowledge, I understood there is nothing more real and deep than love. Becoming love is your higher self, living in fear is your old self. I welcome you onboard this journey of meditativeness, healing and manifesting the highest of desires by feeling the power of love, oneness, compassion and gratitude.

Jordan Peterson, a famous Canadian Psychologist, Author & Media commentator, was asked in a recent interview,

What is real in this life?

Matter is real (knocking his knuckles on the table)

Ok, that's one answer,

What's real?

What matters is real,

If that's how you act, and that's different than matter, what is the most real of what matters?

How about pain,

Why is it the most real?

Try arguing it away, good luck!

So pain is the fundamental reality?

Alright. Well that's rough!

Doesn't that lead to nihilism and hopelessness?

Yeah doesn't it lead to a philosophy that is unethical towards being??

The most fundamental reality is pain?

Yes,

Is there anything more fundamental than pain?

Love,

Really?

When you are in pain, love and truth, that's what you got?

And you know, if they are more powerful than pain, than they are the most real things.

———◆———

LIST OF PROGRAMS & WORKSHOPS OFFERED AT ARF HEALING SCOPE

EMBRACE THE SUPER HUMAN ~

This program is designed for people seeking wisdom with in themselves. It is also for people who feel stagnated in their lives and are looking for a major leap in their Physical, Mental & Spiritual growth, it is also for people who are suffering from chronic illnesses or have fought out of major diseases and ailments and are looking for rejuvenating their lives. It is also for people who are fighting the after effects of the pandemic like warriors and seeking to craft and manifest a future they deserve.

As I believe there is no Coaching without Teaching, this course is for people who are ready to see beyond their veils of perception and ego and are dedicated to embracing the teachings delivered in this program. It encapsulates different teachings of modern sciences and ancient theologies, hugely inspired by the work of many renowned Scientists, Leadership experts, Gurus & powered by the science of Neuro Linguistic Programming (NLP).

"Embrace the super human" is a program that is designed to help you dive into your own being, and recognize the super human potential you hold with in. Embracing the super human in you is the first step to creating your reality. It teaches you about the hidden potentials the human body hosts.

This program will help you clear major blockages in your mind stored in terms of negative emotions and damaging beliefs using the arts of Neuro Linguistic Programming therapies. These negative emotions and damaging beliefs are mostly the reason for hindering manifestations you have been desiring to receive.

As this program rearranges your understanding about the "Law of Attraction" with the help of modern science, You will come to an understanding that these emotions and beliefs you have stored in your mind, due to bad experiences in life, are a product of a neuro logical pattern in your brain and these patterns are what stands the biggest wall between you and your manifestations. Healing the subconscious mind with the power of Neuro Linguistic Programming is merely magic and the same has been proven by changing lives of millions & millions of people over the past four decades across the world, with countless success stories of people manifesting abundance of wealth, healed tumours and cancers, to manifesting their soulmates and twin flames. It is because once we cleanse the subconscious mind the wall between you and your manifestations collapses, and clears its way to attract what you desire and deserve. The personalized meditation in this program is designed to help you reach the eternal present moment effortlessly and craft your life by your conscious will. Today you stand a conscious choice away from choosing a life you deserve

AWAKEN THE SUPER HUMAN ~

This program takes you to the depth of your soul, and teach you the extraordinary science of the brain and the heart connection and the significance to physical and nonphysical reality, and to healing the mind, body and spirit. It takes you on a journey of exploring modern science in regards to the seven chakras or energy centres of our body and its connection to every major gland of your body. It explains the connection of the energy body and the physical body and how to gain harmony between the two.

After you have embraced the hidden potentials in you, you proceed to unleashing it unlocking it with in you. With mountains of knowledge and wisdom to learn from this program, You are also presented with three most important meditation rituals personally designed suiting your energies that will help you cleanse your physical, mental and spiritual body and make you experience life from a beautiful start. This program is designed to venture every corner of your subconscious mind and do the necessary repair and healing using the arts and science of Neuro linguistic programming and replace every un-resourceful habit, behaviours and emotion with resourceful intelligence. If you have hated science all your life like me, I can assure you that you are going to love it and its relevance to your physical and spiritual life.

ARF MASTER COACH CERTIFICATION PROGRAM ~

Becoming a life coach is not a career one chooses, but this career chooses one for its service to reaching humanity, more than a career it's a calling. It's a calling one gets when he or she has suffered tremendous amounts of pain or was just born for a purpose to serve humanity.

With the lessons comes wisdom, and with wisdom, there begins a new life, begins a new purpose, when traumas turn into dreams, dreams of healing everyone who is walking on that journey and assuring them they will be fine, makes many of us to jump into the burning desire of helping people on their mental, spiritual and physical grounds. This is where a life coach is born, a call that has been answered by the soul. Money is just the food for our content body, but the experience of helping someone is food for the hungry soul we have. You become a successful life coach by helping people take the best of decisions in their life, help people learn the finer aspects of living a joyful life to building a positive subconscious mind. For me, being a Life Coach, gave me immense amount of happiness, but still left an empty spot in my heart, pushing me higher than my purpose of living this life. It pushed me into great curiosity of knowing this life beyond. It took me for an expedition into some of the most splendid mountain ranges and packed me with amazing goodies of knowledge and wisdom. The Arf Master Coach certification program is designed in a way to help you understand life from three dimensions of our existence and learn the capability and the finer art of delivering this knowledge to the needed souls. Primarily it takes you through a journey of mystical experiences and knowledge which connects this life to our afterlives. Secondly it is designed to make you experience your own mind as if it was placed in your hands, it teaches deeper aspects of quantum science that connects our spiritual world to the physical world through the bridge of our mental world. Thirdly it takes you to a point to meet your physical body. It will help you understand your body in the way of holistic living. A life that will keep your Physical Mental and Spiritual health vibrating high.

The second part of the course will take you through to understanding the finer arts of neuro linguistic programming and its application in our life and our clients and the science behind NLP Psychology. it will teach you the detail of NLP therapies and its will certify you as a NLP Practitioner.

The Master coach program will give you an over the edge experience to your own life and how we can help others take happiness and joy to their after lives. With a mountain of knowledge and wisdom to learn and experience from this course it needs a certain amount of dedication and time. The course is designed for a total of 60 sessions in 6 months. Each session will take a dedication of two hours.

Upon the successful completion of the program, you will get certified as a Arf Master Coach and become a part of the Arf Team of Leaders, Coaches and Consultants and set ablaze your passion and dream of helping everyone in need while you make a million-dollar living.

NLP CORPORATE WORKSHOPS -

At the ARF Corporate workshop Event, you will be going through a three-day training that will help you enhance your Sales pitch, to enhancing your Marketing creativity and performance. It will take you through a series of interactive training programs where you are taught to build a long-lasting rapport with your clients, colleagues and family. You will be going through multiple modules outlined in the NLP communication and therapeutic science.

NLP FOR SELF CONFIDENCE AND GOAL MANAGEMENT -

This module is designed to help you gain self-confidence to achieving your goals and help you recognize the goal or outcome you are marching for. Lacking a clear vision of the goal can leave one stagnant in their aspirational career. ARF module of coaching in this paradigm will train you to acquire the necessary skill set and abilities envisioning you're Goals using the Arts of Neuro Linguistic Programming.

NLP FOR PHOBIA CURE-

We all develop specific types of phobia's while growing up, and ninety percent phobias root down to our childhood. A few studied by NLP Psychology are Acrophobia (Fear of Heights), Achluophobia (Fear of darkness), Aviophobia (fear of flying), Dromophobia (fear of crossing roads), Arachnophobia (fear of crawling insects), Hydrophobia (Fear of water) and the list goes on to phobias like stage fears and public speaking. Phobias get imprinted as patterns in our subconscious minds and fire every time a similar experience is encountered physically or even just mentally. The cure for phobias is a minuscule of any treatment medical science can offer. The art of NLP is designed to remove any such compelling pattern in your subconscious mind with the power of Linguistic Programming.

NLP FOR OVERCOMING BAD MEMORIES AND DAMAGING BELIEF SYSTEMS-

As we all grow up, taking some decisions, leading to bad experiences and heart breaks, leaves an imprint as a pattern in our subconscious mind thus turning them into pain full programs of misery when ever encountered with similar incidents. Most of the times life is not so bad, but blending the present experience in with something more disastrous that happened in the past, we tend to suffer a multitude more for unnecessary reasons. The pain is often stored as a bad memory and starts effecting every part of our lives if not attended to in a healing manner. The art of NLP works with an approach called timeline therapy, where the practitioner will take you down to beginning of the damaging memory or belief and virtually disconnect the neural pathways that goes to your brain into a pattern stored in your subconscious mind, and set you free from the cycle of misery and suffering it had entangled you with mentally. The ARF NLP timeline therapy and meditations are designed for the same purpose and has helped countless beautiful beings live far more fulfilling lives than before.

NLP FOR SPIRITUAL LIFE AWARENESS –

Wonderfully said by every philosopher and Guru, "to taste one drop of spirituality, one has to shut down the chatter in their mind". A distracted mind that runs on an average of 60-100 thoughts per minute will never let one reach a point where a mind becomes still, a point where the physical body, mental body and the spiritual body hold a conscious awareness equally. Stillness is achieved with a conscious practice of meditative activities. Meditation is simply a ritual we use to acquire a chatter free mind. At ARF we host various different types of NLP powered transcendental meditations to help you raise your awareness from physical to mental to the spiritual body. As well said by Dr. Joe Dispenza, the ultimate strive for a human being should be to evolve from "someone" to "no one" to "everyone" speaks volumes about the power a human body holds when operating multidimensional in a state of "Wholeness".

NLP FOR EFFECTIVE PARENTING-

Children are sacred, Sacred for every reason we can think of, they are divine beings who need to be nurtured in the most self-empowering ways, as we know children are in a state of hypnosis till they reach the age of eight. Every word and command delivered to the child leaves a lifelong imprint of a pattern in his subconscious mind barely without any effort. At ARF NLP Effective Parenting Courses and Workshops we teach deeper aspects of a child's psychology in terms of linguistic programming. When you know your child is on an auto programming mode till the age of eight, why not help your child with imprinting the strongest values that helps him live from an early age a joy full, happy and a content life, with the help of your language, skills and actions.

NLP FOR LONG LASTING RELATIONSHIPS-

Living in today's world being utterly satisfied with every person we encounter is an impossible thing to map, leaving alone our better half. Most of the relationships fail not because of anything real but purely abstract events occurring in between two people, and fall apart due to improper communication. As defined by the science of NLP that every human operates on three major communication modules. They are called Visual representational system, Auditory representational system and Kinaesthetic representational system, in short it is called VAK. What the system means is that some of us use visual representation as our primary source of analysing outer environment and information and some use Auditory or Kinaesthetic representation as their primary source. The clash between two people in any relationship is caused between two representational systems, not actual people. Never the less two fall apart sooner or later due to the mismatch in their communication modules. At ARF NLP Relationship Coaching, the finer aspects of balancing these communication modules in your life to experience more happier and blissful relationships is crafted in the most simplistic ways.

NLP WORKSHOPS FOR SCHOOLS AND UNIVERSITIES-

At ARF Careers and Education events, you will be taken through series of modules which primarily helps you gain focus to what you are aiming at in life in terms of career, dreams and Goals. With ARF's dedication to crafting young visionaries, this three-day event is designed for a complete paradigm shift in your studies, careers and every social relationship.

Post completion of the Workshops, you will be given a Course Certificate of completion by ARFHS~NLP and accredited under a certified NLP Practitioner member of ANLP India (Association of Neuro Linguistic Programming).

———•———

Printed in Great Britain
by Amazon

32060290R00116